Praise for Martin McKenzie-Murray

'As my speechwriter and policy adviser, Martin McKenzie-Murray made our world a better place with his insight, his empathy, and his passion. In *A Murder Without Motive*, he brings these skills to the story of Rebecca Ryle, at the same time brilliantly challenging the tsunami of brutality and banality that male culture can be. This powerful book gives us a glimpse of a vibrant and much-loved daughter, sister, and friend — and I challenge any parent not to be touched by the courage, resilience, and generosity of spirit shown by Fran and Marie Ryle.

'At the time of her death, one man stripped away Rebecca Ryle's dignity. In some small way, those involved in the telling of this story have reinstated that dignity with love, thoughtfulness, and a passion to challenge the status quo.'
— Ken Lay, former chief commissioner, Victoria Police

'Martin McKenzie-Murray is a writer of exceptional moral heft. He assays pain and loss with an intimacy few others achieve, never losing sight of the humanity that blooms around trauma. As a journalist, his great project is the unexplainable. Nowhere is that project explored with more clarity than in this book. He feels and is felt on every page.'
— Erik Jensen, editor of *The Saturday Paper* and author of *Acute Misfortune: The Life and Death of Adam Cullen*

A MURDER WITHOUT MOTIVE

Martin McKenzie-Murray is *The Saturday Paper*'s chief correspondent. He is a former Canberra speechwriter, political columnist for the *Age*, and adviser to the chief commissioner of Victoria Police.

A MURDER WITHOUT MOTIVE

the Killing of Rebecca Ryle

MARTIN MCKENZIE-MURRAY

SCRIBE

Melbourne • London

Scribe Publications
18–20 Edward St, Brunswick, Victoria 3056, Australia
2 John St, Clerkenwell, London, WC1N 2ES, United Kingdom

First published by Scribe 2016
Reprinted 2016

Earlier versions of parts of this manuscript have appeared in various publications, including *The Drum*, *Lifted Brow*, *King's Tribune*, and *The Saturday Paper*.

Quoted material on p. ix from 'Soon Enough' by The Constantines, reprinted with the kind permission of GalleryAC Music; on p. 9 from *The Journalist and the Murderer* (2012) by Janet Malcolm, reprinted with the kind permission of Granta Books and Janet Malcolm.

Typeset in 12/16pt Adobe Caslon Pro by the publishers

Printed and bound in Australia by Griffin Press

 The paper this book is printed on is certified against the Forest Stewardship Council® Standards. Griffin Press holds FSC chain of custody certification SGS-COC-005088. FSC promotes environmentally responsible, socially beneficial and economically viable management of the world's forests.

Scribe Publications is committed to the sustainable use of natural resources and the use of paper products made responsibly from those resources.

9781925321357 (Australian edition)
9781925228618 (UK edition)
9781925307511 (e-book)

CiP records for this title are available from the British Library and the National Library of Australia

scribepublications.com.au
scribepublications.co.uk

For Rebecca

'Years from now, they will make water from
the reservoirs of our idiot temper / Soon
enough, work and love will make a man out of
you.'

— 'Soon Enough', Constantines

'You've got yourself involved in something big,
young man.'

— Detective Sergeant Terence Rakich

CONTENTS

Introduction 1

One   The Dunes 19

Two   Peek-a-boo 45

Three Boys Will Be Boys 67

Four   The Boat 77

Five   Speak Softly and Carry a Big Stick 123

Six   The Pebble Men 163

Afterword 197

Acknowledgements 221

INTRODUCTION

We were eating breakfast in McDonald's when my parents told me they were going to Rebecca's funeral later. I wished they'd said something earlier. I wanted to go, but I wasn't dressed properly: T-shirt, distressed jeans, filthy canvas sneakers. My cultivated slackness was completed by long, greasy hair — an emulation of my art-heroes, The Beatles — and doubtful patches of facial hair. I had just returned from a quixotic spell teaching in South Korea, where I'd been delaying the real and imagined strictures of adulthood. It was 2004, and I had just turned 23.

When I returned, everyone was talking about the murder. I had temporarily moved back in with my parents in Perth's northern suburbs. A week before, just a few streets away, a young woman's body was found on the grounds of the primary school. Rebecca Ryle had been strangled, her body found at sunrise and damp from sprinklers. Her cardigan was torn, her bra twisted, and her pants flung up onto a classroom roof. Her pink underwear lay beside her, and the scene was dotted with the contents of her handbag: ATM receipts, hair scrunchie, broken sunglasses. Rebecca Ryle was 19, and her home was just 50 metres away — the length of a swimming pool lay between her body and her front door.

My parents hadn't known Rebecca Ryle or her family, but my brother knew the man who had already been charged with her murder. Cameron had known James Duggan for years. They were both 19, and had once chugged beer in car parks and pulled bongs made with punctured Coke cans. They had once joined house parties swollen with aggression, where one's personal worth was expressed by a capacity to withstand or commission violence.

They had never liked each other. They had, in fact, grown mutually contemptuous. Years later, Cameron would tell me, 'It wasn't long before I figured out he was someone I didn't want to be friends with. He was a bit loopy. But for the next five or six years he was still friends with my friends, so I was always in contact with him, one way or another. As far as I was concerned, I didn't like him, and he didn't like me. We were quite honest about it. Of the people we were hanging around, and the sort of environment it was, everyone had their tough-guy acts on, but after getting to know people, that would sort of break down. But with him it never did. He never seemed right to me.'

Cameron and James orbited each other anxiously,

tethered by peer groups and suspicion. My brother despaired of his mates' tolerance of him. The last time Cameron saw him, James had uttered some sullen obscenity at him. Cameron turned and felled him with a punch. 'I was standing over him,' he told me. 'James sort of cowered, and everyone else laughed, and I remember someone else saying, "I told you he was a pussy", because he always had this guard on; but when it came down to it, he stayed on the ground. And that let me know he was a lot weaker than he put on.'

Cameron hadn't seen James for almost two years when he heard about the killing. He was on a bus heading home to Mum and Dad's that was tracing its way around the school. The scene was teeming with authorities, and the bus's usual route was blocked. As it made its detour, Cameron stared curiously at the police tape. He realised what he'd seen when he watched the six o'clock bulletin that evening. 'James was the first name that came into my head when I heard. And I said that to a friend of mine. I saw it on TV, and my friend called straight after. There was certainly shock. James had popped into my mind, but … it's a natural reaction to guess when you hear it's someone your own age who lives down the road, but I guess I didn't really believe it could've been him, even though I had guessed it was.'

The murder aroused tender instincts among locals, and the proximity of the victim's home became a source of sombre astonishment. The Ryles' front lawn was quickly carpeted with bouquets, and they were brought meals by neighbours. If the murder hadn't quite galvanised the community, it provided a melancholy focal point. The local newspaper shared the Ryles' decision to hold a public funeral, and my parents felt obliged to attend and bear witness. In retrospect, it was touching. My parents aren't very social. Growing up, I don't recall any sermons about the importance of community. In fact, I suspected that 'community' for them was an irritatingly vague and fatuous concept. But in McDonald's that morning, they surprised me with their commitment to this imagined community and to subtly enhancing the dignity of Rebecca with their presence.

The fact we were in McDonald's appalled me. It was a reminder of the casual vulgarity of the suburbs I had once escaped: first, via university; second, by the more elaborate rejection involved in moving to an outer district of Seoul. I was bothered by the white noise of the wastelands — a studied indifference to culture and enlightened ambition. I was *of* these suburbs, but the very thing my parents had desired for me — a university education — had transformed me into a relentless and obnoxious critic of them. They were unimpressed with my cultural cringe, and how it implicated them. I was an awful snob. And as I sat there eating my sausage and egg McMuffin, I assumed that this vast ocean of banality had somehow contributed to Rebecca's death. James's milieu had been mine.

I was supercilious. My thinking went something like

this: McDonald's represented immediate and witless pleasure. And in my head, it was all messed up somehow with high school, which, with a few years' hindsight, I now detested as a locus of bigotry, boredom, and violence. It was also much more than that, of course — often quite safe and stale and normal. While my brother knew James Duggan, I thought I knew many just like him — dull kids content to practise their cruelties in car parks and at house parties. Here were the Badlands: a place not materially impoverished, but haunted by low expectations. Homeowners might have been shocked by the killing, but my brother and I weren't. Cameron had been whipped with bike chains, nearly run over, and had seen his mate's head scrambled with a baseball bat.

My theory of the killing as a symptom of a broader psychic despair was startlingly pretentious. I had adopted snobbery and cultural theory to misdiagnose whole expanses of suburbia. I had mistaken my rebellion for insight. And never mind that there were murders in the inner-city suburb I would soon move back to. That nearby corners were bubbling with addicts and streetwalkers, or that I had been jumped by four guys a block from home, their bejewelled fists remaking my face. All this was just colourful embroidery, a part of the cherished, edgy dynamism of my new neighbourhood.

I wasn't sure what to do. I wanted to attend the funeral — like my parents, I felt the pull of obligation — but thought that my clothing was improper, even offensive.

There wasn't time to go home and change. My brother was in a worse position. Cameron knew his presence might cause trouble. Many who had known Rebecca at Mindarie Senior College now loathed the Clarkson High kids associated with her alleged killer. At a house party not long after the murder, old friends of Duggan's — who were now furiously renouncing their past friendship with him — were confronted by some Mindarie boys. 'It nearly turned into a brawl,' my brother remembered. 'There was that sort of tension for a while. People were scared to be associated with him.'

Cameron knew that his longstanding suspicion of Duggan — and his assault of him — wouldn't be known to the aggrieved at the funeral. The Mindarie College boys might recognise Cameron merely as a Clarkson boy, and assume an automatic connection with Duggan. Questions of punishment and honour are not well answered by grieving boys.

I went to the funeral. The chapel was full with about 300 people, and I stood discreetly among a large group of mourners at the back behind the pews. At the front was a projection screen upon which were beamed images of Rebecca. She was smiling in most of them. As we stared at the photos, one of her favourite songs played: 'Wonderwall' by Oasis.

What to say of a funeral for a teenage murder victim? The hushed solemnity of the congregation rubbed weirdly against the shared feeling of obscenity. There were no answers here — just a macabre numbness, through which the community bore witness. While the Ryles consoled each other, I shuffled out with my parents and exchanged platitudes. What else was there to do?

After the funeral, I took the train back to the city and walked a few blocks to a pub. I ordered a beer, sat down, and opened my notebook. Then, like the reporter I desperately wanted to be, I scribbled down descriptions: of the church, the mourners, the mood. Then came my lofty exegesis about the psychic bruising of the suburbs — the work of a young man desperate to interpret the crime as a matter of literary significance. It wasn't the work of a serious journalist, of someone who meets with the multitude of people involved, and studies the relevant documents. This was reverse-engineering: I was starting with a grand but vague assumption, and working back to the murder from there.

The work was quickly abandoned. But the story stuck. When I revived it eight years later, I could see that it was far more interesting and brutal than I'd realised. And while my 23-year-old self embarrassed me, I wasn't that wrong. There *was* something about these suburbs, and I came to think that it had played both subtle and overt roles in the death. Nor could I disentangle it from my adolescence.

I finally met the Ryles in November 2012, nearly three months after first making contact with them. Eight years had passed since the funeral. I met them at their home, the one across from the park — the one Rebecca used to live in. They couldn't have guessed how much I had thought about them — how often I'd wondered about their recovery, and why they had stayed in the city, the suburb, the *house*. They couldn't have known about the times I woke in a sweat, snapped from surreal reconstructions of the murder.

I had joined Facebook to find them. I studied their photos of parties and holidays. The profile of Chris — one of Rebecca's brothers — included references to literature and politics. But among this, you had to strain to detect the calamity. I wanted to make real contact, and spent hours finessing my private message to them. But what would they think? I was self-conscious, worried they might consider my interest glib or fleeting, a sickly counterpoint to the depth and longevity of their pain. My message would feel like it had come from nowhere. Years had passed. Newspapers had abandoned the case. And here was a journalist announcing his intention to write a *book* about them. I didn't think I was a reporter so much as a cheap prankster-god launching bolts of inquiry from the ether. What if these bolts reanimated their grief? I paused for minutes above the 'send' button, obsessively scouring the message for spelling mistakes. I thought any errors would be thick with significance for the recipients. Evidence of indolence or indifference.

I promised to treat the story with the respect Rebecca deserved, and I meant it, but I didn't yet know what forms that respect would take. I never imagined how involved I would become.

Not long before I contacted the Ryle family, I read Janet Malcolm's book *The Journalist and the Murderer*. She opens with this famous excoriation:

> Every journalist who is not too stupid or too full of himself to notice what is going on knows that what he does is morally indefensible. He is a kind of confidence man, preying on people's vanity, ignorance or loneliness, gaining their trust and betraying them without remorse. Like the credulous widow who wakes up one day to find the charming young man and all her savings gone, so the consenting subject of a piece of nonfiction learns — when the article or book appears — his hard lesson. Journalists justify their treachery in various ways according to their temperaments. The more pompous talk about freedom of speech and 'the public's right to know'; the least talented talk about Art; the seemliest murmur about earning a living.

What was *my* justification?

Dear Marie,

Allow me to introduce myself: my name's Martin McKenzie-Murray and I'm a political columnist for the *Age* newspaper in Melbourne. Previously I worked as a speechwriter in Canberra. The reason I'm writing to you is that I'm working on a book on the death of your daughter, Rebecca. I'm from Perth originally, and my parents have lived in Mindarie for some years now. In fact, I attended the funeral of your daughter, though I did not have the pleasure of knowing her.

I would like to make clear that I'm a respected political columnist and writer — I am not a trashy tabloid hack, and I have no interest in writing a shallow or salacious story. Nor do I have any interest in cynically using what must still be a considerable pain for you and your family.

What I am interested in, and what the book's real focus is, is how individuals and institutions make meaning of tragic and senseless acts. I'm interested in your thoughts on justice and psychology and I'm interested in how you have coped — and I'm interested in writing something which will suitably honour your loss.

I think it's true to say that most of our crime reporting is slim and trashy with no interest in deeper stories. I want to write an intelligent and respectful book. I want to tell a story that does your daughter justice, drawing intricate profiles of the many people and institutions involved in such a tragedy as struck your family — and how each makes their own meaning with their own rules and philosophies.

I would be grateful for an interview with yourself and your family, Mrs. Ryle. I think it would be of great importance to the book. It would be a stronger book.

I understand this must be quite a surprise for you, and you will wish to think about it deeply.

I now live in Melbourne, but I am very happy to fly to Perth to meet you at a time and place that is convenient for you.

It would be a pleasure to meet with you.

Kindest regards

As I waited for Marie's response — unsure of what I'd started — I provided my own supporting evidence for Malcolm's contempt: while I was concerned about what scabs my message may have scratched, I instinctively wondered at what point the book was doomed for lack of access. My sympathy was mixed with calculation. *What happens if they don't agree?* Then I would admonish myself for the vulgarity of these instincts, and brood repentantly.

A month passed. I did not intend to inquire about the delay. After all, I had proposed to make their private grief public. They would have as long as they needed to think about it without interruption.

And then, an email arrived:

Hi Martin,

Sorry it has taken us so long to get back to you but as you can imagine it was a bit of a bolt out of the blue sort of thing. We have had a few long discussions about the book with family and friends and have come to the conclusion that we would like to talk to you although there are a couple of questions I would like to ask ...

I was exhilarated. I'd made contact. They had thought hard about their response, had sought counsel from their friends and family. They had anticipated the risks to their hearts and reputations, and had tried to divine my intentions. They had little to go on. Until we met, there was still a gulf between us, albeit one bridged by a mutual interest in telling Rebecca's story. But what was that story? There was still so much mystery and irresolution. Among the people I anticipated speaking to, I couldn't assume a consensus solution. There would likely be gaps and contradictions — stories that conflicted with the Ryles'.

But first there were Marie's questions of me:

What made you chose Rebecca as your subject?

Why Rebecca? Of course they'd ask this. Why not some other murder, infamous or otherwise? Or the still-unresolved serial killings in Perth? Why, long after the police tape had been withdrawn and the children had gone back to school, was I interested now?

A few things, mostly personal. My parents live in Mindarie, and have done for some time. I grew up mostly in Sorrento, but my younger brothers and sisters lived in the area, so attending Mindarie College (though they did not know Rebecca). So, I know the area well and was appalled by the tragedy that befell your family. Like I wrote earlier, I think, I attended Rebecca's funeral.

Second, my brother knew Duggan. They were social enemies, of a sort. They had mutual friends but also a mutual dislike for each other — my brother Cameron was often telling his friends that they shouldn't trust him. In fact, the last time my brother ever saw him (many years ago) he had a physical confrontation with Duggan.

Third, I'm interested in how individuals and institutions of justice make meaning — that is, what they decide is important and what isn't; how they make sense of the senseless; where the expectations of individuals affected by such a tragedy are similar to the expectations of justice, and where they diverge. Meaning is important to the story, and I was struck by the sentencing remarks (peppered by the words 'mystery' and 'enigma') which suggested a heartbreaking mystery. How do we determine the answer to 'why' and what happens when we can't answer it satisfactorily? Naturally, you may have very firm answers to this, which would, of course, be reflected.

The second question was inevitable, and much harder to answer:

Will we have the option to proofread what you have written and amend if necessary?

A quick way to find the mainline of media ethics is to ask: whose story is it? But trace it and you don't find the heart of the thing, but a spaghetti junction of claims. For the Ryles, the answer is obvious: it is *their* hell, and *their* story. Their suffering bestows a moral authority, invulnerable to the journalist's sense of entitlement. The Ryles' position is pure and self-evident: *This is quintessentially ours, because we feel this pain and you merely think about it.*

I knew how skeletal my interest was, in contrast. The sum of it was: my brother knew the man charged with Rebecca's murder, and the case had been a portal of periodic reflection on my adolescence. My interests were obtuse and indulgent. I was peripheral. And yet I was making a serious claim to be the person to write it. But if we fiercely patrol those borders — if we accept that only the people involved in acts themselves are permitted to write or authorise them — we would tell fewer stories, would have bookshelves filled exclusively with anointed and anodyne histories. I went ahead with my initial inquiries.

In the end, there is nothing pleasurable in explaining journalistic independence to a bereaved family. I replied:

A completely reasonable request, with a delicate answer: it's important for writers and journalists to balance fairness, accuracy and thoughtfulness on one hand, while maintaining their independence on the other. However, I fully appreciate your apprehension at placing your faith in a stranger, and I would make sure that all transcripts of my interviews would be made available to you so you can check for accuracy, and add or remove anything as you feel necessary. I must stress that this isn't a normal process for journos — independence is a core ethic of the job — but I'm happy to do this given your sense of vulnerability and the gravity of your pain. I'll also be in Perth shortly, and for some time, so I'm happy to meet as frequently as possible (if you'd like) so you can develop an understanding of me, and the book. You can feel free to call me whenever, also. My mobile is: xxxx-xxx xxx.

I would become more flexible, but much came before I did.

The night before I met the Ryles, I was in a bar in the city. I was anxious, but the Ryles felt worse. They were at home, on the same couches from which they had farewelled their murdered daughter, debating the costs and benefits of confession. I was with callow friends of friends who were ironically comparing the health warnings on their cigarette packs. The contrast between their glibness and my preoccupation was jarring. Those tattooed bartenders, who bragged about mixing cocktails in baked-bean tins, industriously mocked the burghers of the northern suburbs for their supposed vacancy, greed, and unwitting celebration of sterility. And goddamn if I wouldn't have once joined them. In 2004, I *was* them.

I sullenly nursed another beer, realising my irritation was deeply personal. 'It's up there in those suburbs,' I wanted to shout, to them, but also to my younger self, 'that the Ryles live voluntarily in the shadow of death.' Even before I met the Ryles, I had become intensely defensive of them. I was betraying my own anxieties.

I didn't sleep well that night, and neither did the Ryles. I woke doubtful and jangled, made coffee, and studied the train timetable. Then I agonised over my clothing, trying to secure an imaginary place between professionalism and endearing informality. While I was doing this, Marie Ryle was furiously vacuuming her house to allay her nerves.

I took the train up north to what was then the end of the line, a 40-minute journey to Clarkson station. It's the transport hub for freshly reclaimed sand and brush, which now accommodates a sea of brick houses. At the station, kids in basketball singlets were swigging energy drinks with studied nonchalance. They seemed to own the station, declaring that ownership with their indifference to train times. The station's traditional purpose wasn't theirs.

I waited for a bus — the same bus, perhaps, that my brother took eight years ago past the school. Except that *my* bus didn't arrive. I looked at the time and began to panic. I didn't have long to get there. I called a cab, muttering irritable prayers for its arrival. The Red Bull I'd drunk to paper over my fatigue wasn't helping. I paced up and down the car park, but the cab came, and it was only a short ride to the house where Rebecca once lived. There was a gently ascending brick driveway. A modest car with a Bolton Wanderers sticker on the back was parked out the front, alongside a small patch of buffalo grass. A narrow road separated it from the school, the oval, and the small metal plaque of remembrance for Rebecca.

I took a deep breath and knocked on the front door.

ONE
THE DUNES

Fran Ryle was tired. Of the weather, the pessimism, the 12-hour shifts at the power plant. He was tired of the schools — 'sausage factories', he called them — and their grey complacency. He was tired of the blokes in the pub and their dull, laconic rituals. He was tired of Bolton, of Lancashire, of England. It felt as if the whole country were sagging.

Fran was short and thin with an open, kind face. He had large ears and a large nose, and cropped brown hair. He was gentle. His speech was articulate and impassioned, voiced with a working-class Lancastrian accent, as thick and comforting as gravy. Fran had left the Royal Navy a few years earlier, where he had served for more than a decade as a mechanic. Serving Her Majesty, Fran had fought in the Falklands and seen the world. Now he was an engineer at the local power plant. It was the start of the new century.

While gentle, Fran possessed an old-fashioned flintiness. His mother was born to a stern father in 1932, and inherited his distaste for broadcasting emotion. She spoke little of her feelings. When Princess Diana was killed, she simply said, 'That was a sad thing, wasn't it?', but it was a rhetorical question, not an invitation to converse. She viewed the grand public expressions of grief with suspicion, as evidence of a pitiable softness in the new generation. But Fran loved his mother, and she him. Many years later, when the worst happened, she would provide her austere comfort.

Fran's parents divorced around the time Thatcher came to power. After years of distant eccentricity, his father disappeared from their lives. Fran's father had grown up in an orphanage during the Second World War, released at 14 to replace roofs destroyed in the Blitz. He was damaged in some way, and years later Fran and his twin brother would come to suspect their father had been sexually abused in the home. Fran's fiancée couldn't stand him, ever since their engagement party when the old man didn't bring a present. Fran thought the *faux pas* was due to his father's innocent difficulties with etiquette. Marie thought it was bloody wilful.

Fran and Marie met soon after he returned from the Falklands war. Fran walked into a pub, saw Marie, and determined to marry her. He was successful, eventually, but it didn't begin well. On an early date walking through the Lake District, in the north-west of England, an RAF jet screamed overhead. Fran instinctively dropped to his stomach and clasped his ears. Marie wondered what she had got herself into.

They had three children: Rebecca, Chris, and Andrew. The eldest was Rebecca, born in 1985 and a year older than Chris. The two of them were close until about the age of 16, when they drifted apart, but they would come back together on the other side of the world. Andy was much younger, born in 1992.

Marie was tired, too. She worked as a receptionist in a local doctor's clinic, and felt similarly about the leaden sky and ennui. Marie's brother had recently moved to Mindarie — a suburb in Perth, Western Australia — and his sunny dispatches from Oz convinced them to plan a reconnaissance trip for Christmas. They would bring the kids and make a holiday of it.

Mindarie was built on sand dunes and limestone in the 1980s. In its wealth, aridity, and shimmering geology, it resembles a desert mirage in the way of most new coastal suburbs in Perth. The sparse seaside vegetation has been razed in deference to flat-pack mansions, each with assiduously cropped lawns. All of this new wealth is bleached by Perth's peculiarly brazen light.

It's a well-off area — its income comfortably above the national average — and its opulence intensifies the closer you get to the small harbour. Around the water, within swimming distance of the private boats, sit three-storey houses. Some of them look like spaceships. Built on the harbour is Mindarie Quays, a complex housing restaurants, a hotel, a souvenir shop, and two pubs — the

Indian Ocean Brewery and The Boat.

Despite the wealth in Mindarie, the suburbs imm- ediately north and east of it are in much poorer shape. Quinns Rocks to the north, and Merriwa and Clarkson to the east, fare poorly in national rankings of advantage. These are truly the fringe suburbs of Perth, well beyond the end of the northern freeway and still a bit beyond the terminus train station in Butler. As residents continue to prefer living within 15 kilometres of WA's long and glorious coastline, Perth's population map now resembles a snake stretched 90 kilometres north to south. While Perth reaches 50 kilometres east to west — from the Indian Ocean to the Darling Scarp — the overwhelming number of residents live much closer to the beach than the ranges.

Perth's planning is bound to the ocean. It's understandable, but unsustainable. The collective result of these individual preferences for the Perth idyll — proximity to the beach *and* low population density — is a greater metropolitan area absurdly large for its population. Fringe suburbs are pushed further from the city, commercial hubs and transport, and the cost of mitigating this isolation with private travel is severe. This endless stretching creates cultural tundras, where the empty spaces are pocked by detonations of boredom.

Perhaps the most startling thing about Mindarie is that outside of Britain, the suburb has the highest concentrat- ion of Brits anywhere in the world. A third of Mindarie's residents are British, compared with the Australian average of 5 per cent. And it's not just Mindarie. The top seven Australian suburbs with the highest number of Brits are *all* in Perth's northern coastal corridor.

Few homes are without Foxtel dishes feeding English football and *Coronation Street* to the telly. Cars are festooned with stickers of the Union Jack, or its constituent parts — the Crosses of St George, St Andrew, and St Patrick. Go to the local pub, and you'll struggle to see the colours of the Dockers or the Eagles, the two local Aussie Rules sides; rather, you'll see the red or blue of United or Chelsea, Middlesborough or Reading. At the Old Bailey pub in nearby Joondalup, 'colours' are banned, but some of the old shirt-sponsors flow freely — McEwan's, Carlsberg, Newcastle Brown. The Quinns Football Club — 'the Jacks' — wear red, white, and blue, while Joondalup City Football Club is deeply British.

Years ago, I lived on this same coastal strip with my parents. They would later relocate just a little further north to Mindarie itself. Like Mindarie, our suburb had rows of identical mansions, their external brickwork concealed by desert-coloured rendering — apricot, rust, beige — creating a gaudy simulacrum of Tuscany. Up here, new money is like a teenager — desperate for identity and meaningful expression, but guileless in achieving it.

Elderly British relatives came to visit once. Contemplating the size of our house and my Dad's presumed income as a taxi driver, the relative turned his attention to the equally large houses either side of us. 'What does that guy do?' he said, pointing to the house on the left.

'He's a brickie,' Dad replied.

'And that guy?' pointing to the house on the right.

'He cuts lawns.'

'Bloody hell,' my relative said, 'where do the rich people live?'

It is the triumph of the tradie up here, and it confirms Australia's fabled egalitarianism to British visitors. Plenty of the affluence you find in Mindarie is generated by sweat, whether in a booming construction market or mining-related industries — about 20 per cent of Mindarie residents work a trade. Head to The Boat tavern on the marina after work to watch the sun sink behind the horizon, and you'll share it with British chippies, brickies, and sparkies necking Beck's and congratulating themselves on their indecent fortune. Not only have they forsaken their frigid, landlocked cities for a balmy coastal suburb, but they appear to have made the great escape from Britain's lingering class system.

Mindarie is also a conservative place, bucking the strong trend of Perth's northern suburbs voting Labor in state elections and Liberal in federal. Mindarie voting booths reliably endorse the Liberal Party in both. Throughout John Howard's term, Mindarie helped return a Liberal (the moderate Mal Washer) to the federal seat of Moore, and it seemed to me in those years that Mindarie was a neat encapsulation of national complacency and the banality of prosperity. Among the uniform houses, the bleached streets, and palm trees, it seemed as if the greatest public concern was interest rates. The national pastime wasn't cricket — it was playing the property market.

But the greatest public concern depended upon who you spoke to. Down at the Old Bailey, you could overhear British immigrants gravely sharing their anxieties about foreigners 'taking over' Perth. Having colonised Australia once, it seemed these Brits considered themselves exempt from 'foreigner' status. 'You don't want this place to become full of Pakis like London,' they warned.

Still, compared to the small, depressed, and industrialised town of Bolton, Mindarie was attractive. The Ryles visited at Christmas in 2000, and resolved to move permanently. Fran returned to work determined to put in as much overtime as possible to help pay off the mortgage. He spent as much time at the plant as he did at home, while Marie asked for additional hours at the GP clinic.

They arrived in November 2003, and found — by Mindarie's standards — a modest house on a quiet street across from the primary school. It was a brick single-storey with driveway, garage, four small bedrooms. It had an open kitchen, dining, and family area. The light was good, and a glass sliding door opened to a paved area at the side of the house, appointed with a large table and plexiglass roof. At the back was a small pool and a shed. A blonde-brick wall separated them from the neighbours.

From the driveway you couldn't quite see the ocean, but you could smell it on a good day. The water was just a ten-minute walk away. Beside the primary school was a large oval — Abbeville Park — where the students played during meal breaks, and where the Ryles would walk their dogs in the evenings. Sometimes Fran would drag a chair out to the front lawn, open a beer, and watch the sun go down. Taking that first sip was like an emphatic punctuation mark after the statement they'd made by moving here.

I knew this area well. It was where my real education during high school happened outside the classroom. I learnt about suicide when a girl threw herself off a freeway overpass, and learnt about the ineffectual oddities of local politics when that overpass was caged, but the one 200 metres down the road wasn't.

I learnt about grief and the jarring finality of death when friends perished in car wrecks. I learnt about drug abuse when one classmate dropped acid and cut himself up with a razor in the toilets. I saw blood, knives, dope, and the calamitous results of male boredom.

I saw negligent fathers preside sullenly over a small kingdom of beer and football, markers on the road to adulthood. These avatars of manhood sat — fat, idle, and indifferent — on their suede thrones, covering their apathy with the witless tenets of laissez-faire parenting: *Boys will be boys.*

I learnt about sex as some galloped confidently into the breach, while others, like myself, cowered feebly and confected excuses to avoid the loss of virginity. In this, I learnt that the stereotype of sex-ed — of the unstoppable virility of male teens — was a sham, or at least incomplete. Fear trumped desire.

There was one house I visited a lot. Towards the end of high school, the father of my friend bought us booze, and we'd sit out in the courtyard by the pool, sinking VB and talking football. There were rumours the father was having an affair, but the hints of sexual indiscretion didn't seem to embarrass the son. Indeed, they seemed only to reinforce for him the primacy of sexual conquest. Our gatherings were organised around booze, sex, and sport. In my life — or the lives I knew — there seemed to be few hands steering us to other interests.

Among my friends, the common denominator was sport. We played football down in the park, taking turns being keeper in hockey goals. There was no shortage of parks. We'd play foosball in gaming parlours, Subbuteo in family rooms, and FIFA on Nintendo. For a while, we took bodyboards down to the beach. On a good day you could ride an A-frame, created when newer waves combined with the older ones rebounding off the rock wall of the marina — the two movements melding to create a cherished apex. In summer, we rolled our arms over in the cricket nets, or invented our own ball games in the street. On the surface, it was the suburban idyll. But it didn't last. It couldn't.

Within a few weeks of arriving in Western Australia, Fran took the two eldest — Rebecca and Chris — to the local university in Joondalup. He walked into the administration office and asked them how his two children might enrol. They explained the requirement of the Tertiary Entrance Examination, so he enrolled them first at Mindarie College. Rebecca wanted to become a nurse — back home she had volunteered on Sunday mornings at the Bolton Hospice, caring for the elderly — and enrolled in biology, chemistry, drama, maths, and child development. She would make some money working part-time at the local supermarket.

When Rebecca was 14, and the family still lived in Bolton, she'd begun secretly using the landline to call friends on their mobiles. Fran had just left the navy and was working a hard, low-paying job. Then a £160 phone bill arrived. Fran had only made about sixty quid in the week that he received it. He was furious.

'What's the matter, Dad?' Rebecca asked.

'I've worked my bloody arse off for that money!' and he'd taken himself off to the pub to calm down.

But at the start of 2004, things were different. Rebecca was a young woman, and Fran was near ships again. He had found work at the Australian navy's main base on the west coast, the HMS *Stirling* on Garden Island. The base is built on a skinny limestone outcrop five kilometres from the mainland, and linked to it by a causeway. But it was also a three-hour round-trip drive for Fran, bookending a ten-hour shift on the tools mending the destroyers. It was exhausting. One day, after work, Rebecca approached her father: 'I love the way you work hard for us, Dad. I know it's tough, but I really appreciate it.'

Mindarie College had only opened the year before, and sat on a hill overlooking the sea. It was a public school, but was conceived differently — more as a pseudo-tertiary institution, helping its students transition to work or higher education. It existed only for years 11 and 12, and allowed greater freedoms and flexibility for its pupils. There was no school on Wednesdays. For students studying for their university-entrance exams, it was a designated study day, though teachers were available for discussion. For those not sitting the exams, it was a day of vocational work, often as part of work-experience programs.

Students came from all over. Some came by bus from semi-rural Yanchep. Others were refugees from Clarkson High, a school notorious among locals. Some were formerly private-school enrolees. The college had been founded optimistically, and its newness helped develop student camaraderie. Because it comprised students from so many schools, some of the otherwise inevitable inter-school rivalries and cliques were diminished. Students maintained friendships they'd established at their old schools. The Boat tavern — walking distance from the college — became a focal point for this socialising.

Skating and surfing anointed the 'cool' kids. For all the trappings of relaxed, pot-laced civility, the surf kids protected their waves aggressively. Young surfers who 'dropped in' — disrespected the sanctity of the queue and interrupted another rider's wave — would at best be verbally lacerated. At school, students boasted of administering severer punishments. For many teenagers, the mystic tranquillity of the ocean was jettisoned for territoriality. It was just another battleground.

Mindarie College couldn't entirely escape divisions. 'There were tribes, in that the Yanchep kids stuck together,' Katy Warner, one of Rebecca's teachers, told me. 'Then there were the rich kids, the ones with their own jetty. They were mostly of new money, the children of parents doing fly-in, fly-out up at the mines. This was the peak of the mining boom, I think. 2004. And they were the most difficult kids to teach. "My Dad is on ten times what you earn," they'd say. "Why should I care about school?" They knew they didn't even need to finish high school to earn big up there. And then you had the English kids, often from rougher parts of England. It was a mix. But on the whole they were nice kids.'

There was bullying and poisonous recrimination — like at any high school — but there was a prevailing pride and cohesion, too. When the male toilets were first marked with graffiti, it wasn't just the teachers who were appalled. Because the school was new, clean, and humming with a different pedagogy, the defacement struck many students as inexcusable. This was meant to be a fresh start.

If the school was relatively united, there was a marked split between Mindarie and Clarkson. Marmion Avenue was the road that divided them, a 40-kilometre coastal artery that also separated the suburb of my home from that of my high school. On my walk to school, I would leave Sorrento and enter Duncraig through a tunnel burrowed beneath Marmion. The underpass was a traditional site for pre-arranged fights after school. There was a socio-economic disparity between the two suburbs, but not as distinct as that between Mindarie and Clarkson.

It was in Clarkson that the biggest, baddest parties happened — the ones with rich kids and poor; studious kids and graffiti crews; the innocent and the guilty. 'There was a change when you crossed Marmion Avenue,' Warner said. 'Kids came to school with stories of house parties. Awful violence. Places being gate-crashed. They were often Clarkson parties. There was a story from that time of people turning up at homes with baseball bats and destroying the place. The Clarkson parties were dangerous.'

The parties weren't only sites of violence, but of raw sexuality. There were young men who had young women as friends, but, for many, the equation was simple: females were for sex, acquisition, bluster. They were judged relative to how your mates saw them. Guys would pay girls for sexual favours, or 'encourage girls to carry on with other girls for the benefit of the boys,' Warner told me. Her students, not much younger than she was, had confided in her. 'There was an expectation that girls act in certain ways, sexually, at these house parties. Not Becky, I should say. She was older. Mature. But there was definitely a lack of respect for women. There was a sense of entitlement with the boys.'

Rebecca belonged to a gentle group of friends. She was deferential and attentive, and rarely walked past someone in school without smiling. 'She would always say "Hiya" in that real English way they have,' remembered her friend Kat. 'She was incredibly thoughtful.'

Teachers remarked on Rebecca's maturity. She was two years older than her friends, a significant difference at that age. She was both warm and quiet, trying to assimilate in an exotic, sun-bleached place. And unlike some of her friends, she knew what she wanted professionally: to care for children, the sick, or the elderly. She was never in trouble, either with students or teachers. 'She was a happy human being,' Warner told me. 'She was lovely. Gentle. I had a lot of big personalities in that drama class. They would fight for attention. She wasn't like that. She was accepting of everyone. The fact they all liked her was very telling in a high school situation. The girls could be quite bitchy. But she got along with everyone. If people were upset, she sat with them. In her drama class it was all girls. There were lots of tears and hormones. She offered them a shoulder to cry on. It sounds superficial or naff, but she had a good soul.'

It was remarkable, given that Rebecca was homesick. But she worked hard to situate herself gracefully. Much of it came naturally. She had been devouring the works of English crime novelist Martina Cole, and was pressing the books upon friends and teachers. She was also saving her money from her checkout job at the supermarket to travel back to Bolton. Her best friend, Anika, was pregnant. Rebecca wanted to be there when she became a mother.

The Boat was a raucous playground for the overlapping circles of local teenagers, especially on Wednesdays. It was, and still is, something of a tradition in Perth's northern suburbs — that the working week's 'hump day' be marked by drinking. The absence of school on Wednesdays further encouraged the attendance of Mindarie College students. It was a loud collection of students and locals, and there were often skirmishes.

My equivalent was the Breakwater Tavern — walking distance from my house then — which was similar to The Boat in being part of a larger marina, Hillarys Boat Harbour. Wednesdays were the big nights, jammed with underage drinkers grinding lecherously to cover band The J Babies. Their name was a nod to the radio station Triple J, whose staples they so profitably mimicked.

Like The Boat and the house parties, the Breakwater attracted a mix of personalities. We were, for the time being, still yoked together by high school. We all lacked discernment. Wednesdays at the pub were an exciting advanced screening of adulthood, but after graduating I would never see any of these people again.

There were frequent fights, but it was safer there than at the house parties. We were all just that little bit older than before — old enough for us to pretend to be of legal drinking age — and the serious criminals didn't tend to socialise at the tavern. But the place was still swollen with bravado and strains of misogyny. The breathalyser fixed to the wall of the entrance wasn't a public safety tool, but a carnival game. Guys would eagerly insert their straw and blow furiously, hoping for the highest blood-alcohol reading. I watched, lacking the enthusiasm of the others. I was there, but not there — able to fit in without knowing why I really didn't. But for me, as it was for Rebecca, that was it. I had no other friends, contexts, ambitions. I wouldn't develop any until a year into university, when I started reading and volunteering for the student paper. It was all new — I had barely read a book in my five years of high school — but things began to make sense. I discovered latent talents, becoming protective and nurturing of them. I read voraciously. I met friends who were shamelessly strange and skilled and loquacious. Most importantly, I unearthed passion and its benefactors, definition and certitude. It seemed, at 19, that Rebecca was there, too. Mostly aware of herself — what she wanted, what she didn't. She was still nervous, unsure. But she had passion, and that gave her a vision of her future.

These days, friends who knew those suburbs are surprised by my descriptions of them, finding them almost unrecognisable. Back then, they sensed some jagged nerves of teen angst. They saw cars driven by P-platers, the windows trembling with bass. They saw an occasional fight at the train station. But nothing more. And, by any measure, even today, these suburbs *are* safe. The violence was largely discriminatory, committed against peers. It didn't visibly engulf the streets. It was a heavy sub-culture, mostly evanescent for those comprising it, and played out on parallel tracks. But like all sub-cultures, the cocooning effect created a sense of universality. It became normal to buy stature with the currency of violence.

There was a common circuit-breaker, though: graduation from high school. For me, university offered a new culture and different friends. A trade — which was the common choice for my high-school mates — offered money, independence, and discipline. Graduation was a centrifuge, separating those idly associated with the sub-culture from those who were stubbornly fixed to it. But full separation could take a while.

It was in such a world that Rebecca moved, but with much greater optimism, maturity, and focus. She straddled the two worlds, though. Of legal drinking age, Rebecca was nonetheless a high-school student. She had male and female friends, friendships brokered by openness and trust. Many of these friendships began — and were maintained — at The Boat. They were largely good kids, if coarse. They were only 17- and 18-year-olds, slowly but excitedly accruing the effects of adulthood — jobs, cars, pubs. They were transitioning.

From the age of 11, I'd listened to American hip-hop. Incongruously, the first album I possessed was N.W.A's *Straight Outta Compton*, dubbed for me on cassette by an older neighbour. My initial pleasure wasn't musical. It was the thrill of rebellion, of secretly hearing blood-soaked dramatisations of life in South-Central LA. My dad, who almost exclusively listened to Louis Armstrong, Don McLean, and the Glen Miller band, could never know I was listening to 'Fuck tha Police'.

It wasn't long before hip-hop genuinely had me. Track eight on *Compton* was 'Express Yourself', unique on the record for its optimism — in its lyrics, but also in the buoyant bass-line. The song shunned the riotous nihilism of the others, being about the importance of expression and the hypocrisy of artists who cravenly chased success on the 'pop charts'. They were affirming something greater than the right to 'smack bitches' and 'pop gats'. When my parents left the house on weekends, I commandeered their stereo and thrashed it.

When I entered high school, I found others with similar tastes. Early Ice Cube and Ice-T tapes were pirated for me on dual cassette decks, and I furtively played them in my room. Ice Cube narrated the LA riots and promised more; Ice-T dreamt of murdering police. Today, Cube stars in saccharine comedies, while Ice-T *plays* a cop in a major TV series. It was white kids like me who, through a powerful combination of disposable income and radical chic, defanged them and aided their unlikely transformations as members of the entertainment elite. Today, I'm not sure what's worse: the song 'Cop Killer' or *Law and Order*.

Just before I first punched somebody, I listened to Dr. Dre and Snoop Dogg to supercharge my anger. My younger siblings, still in primary school, had told me earlier that James, the kid next door, had teased them. Again. He'd been calling them 'rice eaters' at school — a reference to the fact that, for dinner, we'd often only eat a bowl of rice with a can of Kan Tong sauce dumped on it. Our family's habits and constraints were off limits. I would have to sort James out.

Not long before my kid brothers and sisters told me this, I'd seen James ride past on his bike. I figured, correctly, that he was heading down to Hillarys Boat Harbour. I grabbed my Walkman, jammed in Dre's *The Chronic*, cranked the volume, and marched. I was an acned warrior.

James was doing lazy circles on his bike in the car park, just near the A-frames and The Breakwater. It wasn't fair: I was a small kid, but I had about four years on him. I pulled out my headphones and jogged towards him. 'You talking shit about my family?' He pedalled furiously, but it was too late. I pushed him off his bike and swung wildly. My punch was terrible, skimming harmlessly off his head. He dumped his bike and screamed for help while running towards the Pot Black pool hall. You could often find security guards there. So I walked back home, unsure if I was a hero, a bully, or neither, and shaking with a dim awareness of the dangers of pride and machismo. Then I waited. His family would be over soon.

It was now their turn to defend family honour. I just hoped that James's ambassador wouldn't be his father — a large tradie of few words who I'd been told by James had once repelled burglars with a crowbar. So I was relieved when I saw his mother arrive. She was squat and hysterical, berating me in her thick Yorkshire accent. I don't recall what she said, only her pique. Nor do I recall my response — if I demurred and apologised, or if I was petulantly defensive. My parents didn't celebrate what I did, but they didn't much punish me either. They couldn't stand the family. They wouldn't endorse violence explicitly, but I think it seemed strange to my father to reprimand me for something he privately wished he'd done himself.

Back in school, I floated between cliques. There were those who surfed, those who played football, and those who got high and jammed to Sonic Youth. There were the kids who studied, and the kids in gangs. With the exception of the bright kids, I knew most of them. The description of high school as a patchwork of tribes is a common trope, and can be simplistic. Certainly, there were students who had varied interests and friendships, and some groups were amiable and porous. But in my school the distinctions largely held and, for some, were ardently enforced. Definition was found in opposition.

Among these tribes, music was a signature. Of those who comprised the gangs, those just waiting for the end of Year 10 when the state would no longer oblige their attendance, it was mostly hip-hop and death metal. Not simultaneously, though. There were the shark-eyed skinheads who wore Cannibal Corpse T-shirts beneath their white school polos, and there were those who wore baggy jeans and Wu-Tang shirts beneath theirs. Their differences in musical taste were ameliorated by a shared interest in drugs, violence, and vandalism. The fashion seems amusing now — ridiculous, dated, earnest. But, back then, those uniforms inspired fear.

There were migrations between groups. The son of one of my mother's friends, Ian, was in my year at school. In early high school he was a gifted student, but quiet and shockingly awkward. He drifted. He was wild and impressionable, and he found his identity in being a wind-up toy for the gang members. He shaved off his dense shrub of brown curls, and became a skinhead and connoisseur of death metal and random violence.

He wasn't the largest guy around, but he aroused fear with his unpredictability. He'd drop acid at lunchtime and stalk the corridors, muttering ominously to himself. He wore skinny black jeans and steel-capped boots. In winter, he wore a black trenchcoat. In fact, he may have worn the coat in summer, too. The others in his group used him. They'd exaggerate — or invent — grievances with students, certain they could dispatch Ian to avenge them. And he did. I once saw him pummel a brick wall until his fists bled to psyche himself up to beat a designated target. Unless you were enormous, you'd already lost the fight before you saw him.

His emotional inarticulateness was mirrored at home. His parents' marriage was moribund: his dad's back broken from the effort of plastering a thousand walls; his mother aged from the slog of nursing. There was a sallow exhaustion in that house. It permeated everything. When we visited, I dreaded listening to the latest Sepultura record in Ian's bedroom, where he would try to keep up with the thrashing guitar with his own. Ian's violence didn't spring from an entrenched poverty — except, perhaps, of the ego. It was a far subtler impoverishment, and his raw, malleable soul was banged into violent shape by the purpose he found in the schoolyard and streets. But he recovered. Ian was bright, and last I heard he had gone to university and was in a solid relationship. His younger brother didn't, and slid into heroin addiction, petty crime, and incarceration. I'm not sure where he is now.

Ian was at a house party I went to when we were sixteen. When it finished — having collapsed beneath its own weight of aggression — I was covered in blood and walking a tripping friend home while beer bottles were flung at us. The party had been held very close to our school, and had been prominently advertised through word of mouth. A critical mass of interest developed. Members of different school tribes — and many people outside of them — were geared to go. You developed an acute sense for the potential scale of parties in our high school, and once you'd detected it was going to be huge, vanity compelled you to attend. A party's credibility rested upon how many went, and the more that did, the higher the odds it would descend into madness. It was almost impossible to enjoy yourself at these things, and yet we kept going. The participants were intensely fatalistic. Many were only there to witness bedlam, and to later boast of their bearing witness, and the weight of this expectation almost ensured it. Violence was willed into existence.

From memory, it had been organised by the older brother of a schoolmate. Rumour was he dealt drugs. I had no idea where the parents were. There were hundreds of people, many older and long out of school, and many more from the various graffiti crews that ghosted our suburbs. Hip-hop provided the soundtrack for the carnage. When I arrived, a shatteringly high volume was distorting Cypress Hill songs.

Most people were crammed into the backyard, which you reached via a narrow path on the left of the house. The path was full, too, and people spilt onto the front lawn and the road. This was our equivalent of Truman Capote's Black and White Ball — the event you had to be seen at. It was extraordinary how vulnerable we were to this vanity, which was directly opposed to our personal safety. This party strung together many different individual trajectories, and for most it became the final intersection between those who belonged there, and those who didn't — those for whom a spectacle of aggression was frightening, and those who exalted in it.

I was at the back when the first fight broke out. I don't remember who was involved — I don't think I knew them — but one bloodied guy fell into me, his weight crushing me against a garden rock. I pushed him off, and he went spinning into a group, and I remember one bloke screaming that someone had flung this chap into his girlfriend. Fortunately, it was so crowded that my guilt was initially unclear. Now endangered, and stained with the stranger's blood, I pushed my way back out the front. It must only have been 8.00 pm, and my new football strip — which had cost $100, bought after months of saving my newspaper-round income — was spoilt. I was in two minds: wearing a bloodied shirt usefully suggested to others that it was I who had been fighting. But I was also worried that it was ruined, and that I would have to awkwardly disguise the damage from my parents.

I was on the front lawn now, and people were still arriving, swilling mixed drinks from tins. And then I saw him. Brandon was in his uniform: comically oversized jeans and baseball cap; ink-stained pockets likely containing a bag of weed and a fat black marker. *What the fuck is he doing here?* Brandon was in some crew, and through a botched drug deal, or loan, or theft, or lies, or fuck knows what, had alienated the core group of thugs at the party. Whatever it was, the word was out: Brandon was a dead man. And yet ... *here he was.*

Today, I still suspect that Brandon was infected by the same vanity as I had been. Despite the danger, or perhaps because of it, he was compelled to be seen here. As he approached, I warned him that being there was a very, very bad idea. But it was too late; he never made it across the front lawn. He was set upon by many, his face smashed. As he retreated to the road, he fell and was stomped. His swollen mouth called for clemency, but you could barely hear it for the primal shouts of his attackers.

I remember standing on the lawn, in more or less the same spot in which I had warned him, and watching as a girl brought her stiletto down on his body.

And then: a police siren. The mob retreated. Brandon's busted body was given a reprieve. But the police weren't attending this scene — they were at the other end of the road, dealing with a separate disturbance. Brandon hadn't been saved, and the mob moved back in to finish the job. Brandon would have to save himself. Before they descended, he rose to his feet and stumbled across the road. His attackers waited and watched as he pounded on the door of the house opposite. He was demanding refuge, but the door never opened. As the mob moved towards him, Brandon made a final, desperate decision. Nearly 20 years later, I'm still stunned by my memory of what happened: he sought refuge by crashing through the front window. And that was the end of our Black and White Ball.

None of this happened in slums or public housing. The homes that comprised these battlegrounds were mortgaged, resplendent with pools, gardens, and large TVs. This was the middle class. But livid visions of masculinity played themselves out vigorously. No doubt the smartest kids, the mature kids, saw none of this. They stayed at home, watched movies, started bands. You could easily avoid it if you wanted to. But I didn't. It wasn't until my final year in school, when the place had been vacated of nihilists and thugs, that I resumed — more or less — a slothful but relatively innocent lifestyle of music, booze, and sport.

None of which is to suggest that the boys in these stories foretold their futures with their behaviour. Many — most? — escaped. But these suburbs, charged by pride, boredom, and the rotten aspirations of masculinity, formed a crucible. And within that crucible, the line between doing something stupid and something irreparable was excruciatingly fine. The fatalism, the violence, the thirst for risk, the medieval appreciation of females — most often, these things would play themselves out vulgarly and produce some painfully dull men. They wouldn't often result in death, imprisonment, or serious injury. But these ingredients are common and highly flammable. It's always just a matter of time before chance lights the match somewhere.

TWO
PEEK-A-BOO

On the days when he wasn't working, Peter Carter liked to walk his blue heeler at sunrise. That morning, Thursday 6 May 2004, while his wife was still in bed, he got up and put a leash on his dog. He left his house on Bayport Circuit, Mindarie, at 6.35, and headed up Rothesay Avenue to the park. The sun wasn't up yet, and he liked it that way — leaving in the dark, but returning with the sun fully risen. As he crossed Rothesay to the southernmost part of Abbeville Park, it was beginning to lighten slightly, and he let his dog off its leash. Peter stayed on the path that traced the perimeter of the park, while his blue heeler trotted along behind. As he walked, a woman passed him. 'Good morning,' she said, 'best part of the day.' He agreed.

Peter continued, walking around the oval until it began to bend beside the edge of the school. Demountable classrooms lay on one side of the path; the reserve was on the other. And then, in the grey half-light, he saw her. Her body was face down, her left arm outstretched and her right tucked beneath her torso. She was naked below the waist, her trackpants dangling from a classroom roof, and her pink underwear lying beside one of her legs. ATM receipts were scattered nearby. Peter turned and ran for his dog, and it cowered. 'It's okay, boy,' he said, grabbing a firm hold of the collar. Then, careful to hold his confused dog behind him, he walked close to the body to confirm she was dead. 'The mouth and nose was obscured by dirt,' he later remembered, 'and her flesh was very white.'

Peter didn't have a phone, but knew he had to contact the police. He could see a light on in one of the school buildings, and approached it, still holding his blue heeler. 'Hello? Is there anybody there?' No answer. He continued up through the school, until he saw a man and two women. It was the deputy principal and two cleaners. 'Call an ambulance and the police!' he yelled. 'There's a body down there!' The deputy began to make a phone call, while one of the cleaners broke from the group and ran past Peter towards the body. This wasn't good, he thought. He fixed his dog to a chain fence and took after her.

The cleaner was beside the body now, whimpering uncontrollably. Peter later testified that she was making 'strange' and 'childlike' sounds, and quickly moving her legs up and down, as if running on the spot. Peter grabbed her arm and pulled her away from the body. 'You can't do anything,' he said. By now, the other two — the deputy principal and the second cleaner — had made their way down to the body. Peter was concerned that they were interfering with a crime scene. 'Let's all move to that tennis court,' Peter suggested. 'There's nothing we can do for her. We may as well leave the scene alone.'

They took his advice, and retreated to the court to wait for police. From there, Peter saw the woman he had walked past earlier. She was coming back around the oval towards them. The sun had risen now, and Peter knew she would soon see the body, so he dashed towards her to 'cut her off at the pass'. It was too late. She could see the body over his shoulder, and she began to cry.

First-Class Constable Adam Oswald was another Englishman — tough, burly, and reticent — and he had bought his lot of 'paradise' on Pattani Court, just metres from Abbeville Circle. Whereas Fran Ryle had participated in one of Britain's shortest military engagements, Oswald had served in its longest — Operation Banner, the 38-year deployment of forces to Northern Ireland. During those nearly four decades, the British forces lost 738 members, but were also accused of murdering civilians, including the 13 shot dead on Bloody Sunday. In fact, as First-Class Constable Oswald was preparing for work that morning in 2004, Operation Banner was still three years away from ending.

Oswald had seen death and mayhem in Ulster, and it had prepared him for the emotional quarantines demanded of the police officer. Not that he saw much on the frontline. Oswald was a police prosecutor, spending his time in courts or preparing briefs. That morning, around 6.45, he booked on for work and left in his unmarked car for the Joondalup prosecution branch. On the way there, he was ordered by radio to attend Clarkson police station. When he arrived, he was told there was a '338' at the school — code for a sudden death — and to get there quickly. He was the first officer on the scene. It was about 7.00 am.

Oswald saw that the woman's body was wet — probably from sprinklers the night before — and because she was not wearing any pants, he could see the scarlet patch of lividity on her right hip. Within half an hour to three hours after death, blood is helplessly subject to gravity and begins pooling at the lowest point. Within eight to 12 hours, unless the body has been moved, the post-mortem staining is fully established. Oswald also noted the collapsed system of capillaries, registered as purple splotches and red inflammation, on her neck. He knew he had to secure the scene, so he told those waiting on the tennis court to remain there, assuring them that officers would be with them soon. In fact, other officers were already arriving. Oswald then took out his notepad and made sketches — of the position of the body, the buildings, the oval, the road, and the route he had taken. He noted that her legs were splayed in a V-shape, and that underwear lay beside her. He recorded the fact that there appeared to be no injuries to her head, and wrote that on her left hand she wore a ring and a bracelet. Draped between her legs was a torn portion of her cardigan.

The crime-scene co-ordinator, Senior Constable Blackwood, arrived. Oswald relayed to him his observations, and suggested he take photos of items strewn in the vicinity of the body — scraps of paper, house keys, and a pair of women's shoes. Yellow-and-black crime tape was now being strung around the area, curled around trees and classrooms. Detectives and forensic experts were assembling, but Oswald realised that young students would soon be arriving, too. Those walking to school from the south — across Abbeville Park — would have an uninterrupted sightline to the body. Oswald lived across the road, so he ran home and grabbed a tarpaulin from his shed, came back, and nailed it up between two trees. It obscured the body from the broadest angle of approach. Police members then began shepherding parents and students back to their homes. There would be no school today.

Rebecca wasn't dressed for a big night out — pink cardie and trackpants, her long blonde hair tied up with a scrunchie. She came out from her room and stood at the top of the den where her parents were watching telly. 'I'm off for a walk, Mum and Dad,' she said. It was 8.00 pm on Wednesday 5 May 2004.

Marie was glad — Rebecca's ebullience had returned. The evening before, she had visited her daughter in her room, where she lay melancholically on her bed. 'What's up, Becks?' her mum asked, sliding onto the bed and cuddling her.

'You know, Mum, I just don't feel as if I belong.'

'What do you mean?'

'I don't feel as if I should be here.'

'Of course you belong here, Becks.'

Years later, that conversation still haunts Marie. Hindsight and trauma have transformed Rebecca's words from an expression of homesickness into an awful premonition. But on this night, as Rebecca said goodbye to them, Marie was pleased. Becks had her spark back.

'Don't be late, flower,' Fran said.

At 10.00 pm, just before Fran went to bed, he called his daughter. There was no answer, so he left a message on her voicemail: 'It's your dad here, love. Don't be late, and don't wake me because I've got to be up early. Come home soon.' Fran went to bed, sleeping until his alarm woke him at 5.00 am.

Fran shuffled to the kitchen and flicked the kettle on. Then he checked Rebecca's room. It was still dark, but he could see that her door was open. She hadn't come home yet. *Bloody hell*, he thought irritably, *she better not be partying*. He tried calling her. No answer. He finished his tea, showered, dressed, and walked out to the car on the bricked driveway. The sun hadn't come up yet on the park across the road — it wouldn't for another hour. As he drove down the limestone coast, he wondered where his daughter was. He was furious.

Marie wasn't up much later than her husband. Their son, Andrew, had been marked for possible inclusion in an advanced academic program, and the host school wanted to test him at 7.30 am. Marie roused the boys, then went to check on Rebecca's room. Empty. *Where the bloody hell is she?* She left Chris and Andrew to their breakfast in the kitchen, and stepped outside to the driveway. There was activity across the road — police, reporters. She stood there in her nightie, the sun newly risen, and somehow she knew. *My baby.*

Nauseous, she went back inside. 'What's wrong, Mum?'

'Nothing.'

She tried to eat but couldn't, so she checked Rebecca's room again. It was definitely empty. Marie went back outside. As she stepped onto her driveway, her next-door neighbour Cheryl came out, too, to see what was happening. Seeing Marie, she came over, and together they stared at the police tape and the plainclothes police consulting with each other. Marie walked across the road toward a journalist.

'Excuse me, but what's going on here?'

'They've found a body.'

Marie's throat tightened around her question: 'A 19-year-old blonde?'

'What do you mean?'

'I think my daughter's missing — she didn't come home last night.'

'I'm sure everything will be alright, but just stay there, and I'll go and talk to someone.'

My baby.

The journalist conferred with police, then a detective

broke from the group and approached Marie. His solemnity was a warning. 'Please go back inside your house, and someone will be over soon to have a chat with you.' Cheryl helped Marie back inside — she was trembling now — and put her on the couch from which she had said goodbye to Rebecca the night before. 'Is there anyone you can call?' Cheryl asked. It was after 7.00 am.

Marie called her brother, who lived nearby, and he and his wife drove over immediately. 'Marie, I can't believe this,' he said when he got there. Cheryl left, and as she did, two police officers arrived. 'We'd like some photos of your daughter, please.' As Marie directed them to Rebecca's bedroom, her phone rang. 'Who is it?' asked an officer.

'It's my husband.'

'I'm sorry, but you can't tell him anything.'

Marie stared at the officer while the phone vibrated in her hands. Then she slowly looked down at the phone and pressed 'receive'.

'Hi, Fran.' The police officer studied her, gently trying to appear as if he wasn't.

'Has she come home yet?'

'Not yet, honey, but I'm sure everything's okay. Look, I have to go, love,' and Marie hung up.

At the navy yard, Fran wasn't convinced.

Within their house, there now marched a sombre procession of police, uniformed and plainclothes. Marie stared blankly at them. 'Mrs Ryle?' A female officer came in and extended her hand. 'Detective Deb Wheatley. I'm a family-liaison officer, and I'll help you through all of this, but I think you should sit down.'

It felt then as if the walls, the roof, and the limestone had surrendered their reliability and were closing in on her.

'We think it's Rebecca.'

My baby.

Her phone rang. It was Fran again. He could feel them, too — those things closing in.

We are hopelessly dependent upon clichés to convey psychological violence. We are predictably told that 'nothing can ever prepare you for this', which is true, but it's often just the first in a series of platitudes that comprise the *langue de bois* of trauma. Take Marie: the creeping realisation that her daughter lay dead across the road registered itself with ruthless totality. It's close to impossible to reckon with — much less describe — this scale of disruption.

Shock is profoundly disorienting. Each of us has an emotional map we can occasionally consult. It has discrete territories, and a rich topography. It's complicated and in places shadowy, but — if we're lucky — it's mostly knowable. You can locate yourself on it. And then ... the whole thing goes up in flames.

Another hurdle to expression is the anaesthesia of shock. When you hear the worst possible news, there can be a useful numbness that replaces all of the garden-variety emotions you had previously. It's hard to describe nothing.

The initial shock is intensely physical. It works itself on your intestinal system, creating that 'visceral' sensation — as if your stomach has become a bird sanctuary. You might also feel light-headed, as your orientation dissolves. Familiar things around you — a chair, a tree, a friend — become fuzzy, unfamiliar. You become very weak very quickly. If you're standing, you might fall. You might experience nausea and a sense of claustrophobia. Breathing will be difficult.

The word 'surreal' will be mentioned a lot, which is shorthand for the collision between the prosaic and the catastrophic. Your entire system of concerns is swept away. Now it has to accommodate this One Big Thing. Ordinariness is obliterated, and the contrast between what you were thinking before, and the News itself, is 'surreal'.

What's more, the News has so dominated your body and mind that there is little chance of you being self-conscious about your shock. Self-consciousness has been hijacked, along with your legs and stomach. Not for a little while will you be able to conceive of yourself as a 'grieving person'. At that instant, you simply *are*.

As her phone rang, Marie looked desperately at Detective Wheatley. 'What am I supposed to tell him? I *have* to tell him,' she said, but Wheatley knew her job was to balance gentleness with the need to quarantine persons of interest. 'No, you can't say anything. I'm sorry.' So Marie said nothing, just meekly parried her husband's anxious inquiries. Then she hung up, and faced the alien buzz of the detectives' questions.

Fran couldn't concentrate. He put down his tools, stepped onto the wharf, and lit a cigarette. Something wasn't right. He called Marie again. She answered. 'What's going on, love?' he asked her. 'What's the bloody deal? Where is she?'

Marie stared at Wheatley with wet eyes. 'Okay. You can tell him.'

Marie drew a breath. 'Becky's dead.'

Fran's cigarette fell from his fingers, his legs buckled, and he fell. A workmate ran over. 'What's going on, Franco?'

'My daughter. She's fucking dead.'

In such a moment, a good detective must possess dual qualities: grace as the bearer of awful revelation, and the detached scepticism of a professional who knows that a significant majority of homicides are domestic.* These two qualities may appear starkly opposed, but they're mutually arranged. If a detective isn't sufficiently empathic, he risks not only causing additional pain but also alerting suspects to that other, antithetical quality: hard-nosed suspicion. This might seem morally gaudy, but the successful detective knows that the deployment of his warmer nature provides camouflage for the cooler.

It is a sad and inescapable fact that immediately after

---

* In the 2003–04 reporting period, the period that includes Rebecca's death, only 7 per cent of Australian female homicide victims were killed by a stranger.

a body is discovered, the family exist as a duality: tortured victims and potential perpetrators. They are, until they can be exonerated or charged, like Schrödinger's Cat, and the sensitive detective must have the suppleness to treat them as both at the same time. The idea isn't to condemn anybody. Many detectives I've spoken to emphasise the importance of sensitivity and dignity. The idea is to avoid corrupting leads with sentimentality. You begin eliminating suspects methodically, but you do that as respectfully as possible. It might appear duplicitous — and in some lesser detectives it probably is — but many can at once respect the dignity of the family *and* the investigative procedures.

A police officer drove down to Garden Island to collect Fran, and found him in an unholy state — pale, nauseous, and chain smoking. Workmates gripped his shoulders. The officer introduced himself, and directed Fran to the unmarked car. Colleagues said goodbye, and wondered how they could now work. Fran climbed into the passenger side and asked if he could smoke. The officer nodded and turned the ignition. They had a 90-minute drive up the coast. As Fran stared out at the water, the window down, the detective began gently, with small talk.

'You follow the football?'

'Bolton Wanderers,' Fran answered.

A modest club, not world-beaters. Fran agreed.

The cop drove away from the coast and began gliding

parallel to the Swan River as it wound itself to the city and the northern freeway. As Fran stared at the old brewery on the river's bank, and at the yachts that were sailing beneath a blue sky, he was asked simple questions about Rebecca — her age and school and occupation, ordinary inquiries an acquaintance might make at a party. But as Fran stared out at this gentle scene, it struck him: *He thinks I've done it.* Jolted, Fran began earnestly explaining himself. 'She went out last night. About eight. She said goodbye, we said goodbye. She never came home.' He wept and was incredulous, and the incredulity grew as they turned into the street that bent gently around the school oval. It was now filled with police, and delineated with tape.

The officer pulled into the driveway and helped Fran to the door. Detective Wheatley met him there and introduced herself. Fran looked at her looking at him, and he knew: she was sizing him up. Studying his face, posture, speech. And somehow he knew, too, that her gut was telling her that he was innocent.

Detective Wheatley calmly explained that the police needed to separate them. Marie's brother and sister-in-law were asked to leave, and the husband and wife were questioned in different rooms. The boys were split up, moved elsewhere to be both quizzed and consoled. As family liaison, Wheatley explained the necessity: much as a crime scene is quarantined, so too are the statements made by people of interest. As much as possible, they must be made in a vacuum, untouched by the coercion — wilful or not — of other parties. The separation is not solely to prevent unsavoury collaboration, but to protect our suggestible memories from contamination. Just as stray boots can desecrate a crime scene, so can others traipse through our memories, bending and twisting them. Marie understood, but she was hurt nonetheless. No matter how gentle the explanation, the buried suggestion was obscene.

Between spasms of incomprehension and horror, all four of them told the investigators what they knew. Which wasn't much. *She was a bubbly girl, popular and caring. No, she didn't have any enemies — why would she? She's only 19, for Chrissakes, and we've only been in this country six months. Oh, Jesus. She left about eight last night, said she was going for a walk. We thought she might pop into the pub to see some friends. She was chirpy. Normal. No, she never answered her phone. Oh, sweet Christ.*

Eventually, the investigators left, and the Ryles were reunited in their own home. Detective Wheatley assured them that she wasn't going anywhere. She'd help them through this. Which is when the drinking and magical thinking started, outside at the table on the paved area, right near the pool and Fran's shed. Wheatley sat with them, making sure they were okay, but also ensuring that none of them made a hysterical pilgrimage to the park.

As they sat and cried, Fran tried to trap the detective into an admission of incompetency — that the investigators had blundered terribly, and that the body across the road belonged to some other poor bastard.

He was insistent, prodding at her statements, searching desperately for a weak spot, something that might suggest misidentification. Wheatley was gentle but firm: 'I'm afraid it's Becky.'

George Harrison once said that Beatles' fans may have given their money and their screams, but the members of the band gave their nervous systems. So it is with detectives assigned the family-liaison role. The crime novelist and former New South Wales detective PM Newton told me that if a victim's family 'forced you to be present and witness their pain, you could almost feel resentful — you don't want to be a witness to that much pain over and over again.' At the Ryles' home that day, the psychic fumes were thick and toxic, but Wheatley absorbed it all — as she would for years. She was the opposite of a wedding photographer — professionally obliged to meet strangers on the worst day of their lives.

That Thursday evening, as the sun went down over the Indian Ocean, they were still outside. Except Chris. He was inside getting his gear ready, and he came back to the sliding door to the patio holding his guitar. 'I'm off to the club,' he said.

Each Thursday night, Chris went to the local youth club to jam with friends. Wheatley looked at him. 'You can't go anywhere tonight, mate.' It was shock, of course. A brave but feeble suspension of belief. It was Wheatley's job to remind him. To reintroduce reality.

Fran was at Cape Canaveral when he learnt of Chris's

birth, on a phone in a bar, metres from where the US Navy were retrieving pieces of the *Challenger* shuttle from the Atlantic. Fran's warship had landed at the Cape to refuel and empty its sewage. They were at sea when they listened to news of *Challenger*'s immolation. Then they sailed into the epicentre of America's national shock. It was 1986.

Fran expected to see larger debris pulled from the water — a recognisable section of the rocket booster, say — but while he watched, the divers dredged pieces you could fit in a shoebox. The activity was purposeful; the mood, grim.

Fran knew his second child was about due, but suspecting that neither his nor Marie's messages were reaching each other, he asked to borrow the phone from the bartender. He got through.

'Hello, love. When's this baby coming?'

'I've bloody had it! You have a son.'

'What!'

Fran asked the bartender for the Yellow Pages.

'Why's that, limey?'

'I'm a father!'

'Congratulations,' she said, and the phone directory was handed over. Fran looked up local florists, and ordered a bouquet of red roses to be delivered to Bolton. He bought a beer, and watched the salvage operation.

US space launches were suspended for nearly three years after the catastrophe, and, as it was, Fran and Marie were on the Cape again when *Endeavour* — the shuttle built to replace *Challenger* — made its first launch in

1992. Rebecca and Chris were there, too, as part of a family vacation to Disney World. The family planned to be at the official viewing site for *Endeavour*'s launch, but the mission was delayed because of bad weather. When they heard the rescheduled time, they didn't have much time to drive their rental car to the platform. They didn't make it. They listened to the countdown on local radio while they drove, noticing that all the cars in front of them were pulling over to the side of the highway. They did the same, leaning on the car as they watched. 'Despite the distance,' Fran said many years later, 'the light off it was like a welding arc. You could feel the noise on your ears.' And from the side of the highway, the family watched *Endeavour* bend gracefully around the earth's curvature.

It was almost nine o'clock in the evening. The Ryles were an unstable compound of belief and disbelief. They were frightened of silence, but unsure of how to fill it. Fear and loathing washed their bones: they loathed their daughter's killer, were fearful of all the days following this one. 'Let's get in my car,' Wheatley said. 'We're going to get you some medicine.' And the five of them drove to Joondalup Health Campus, which was full of people, but the Ryles barely noticed. This kind of shock creates solipsists. Nor were the crowds a problem. Wheatley flashed her badge, and the seas parted. It was a swift consultation. Wheatley did the talking, and they left with powerful sedatives. 'These'll knock a horse out,'

Wheatley told them, and she drove them home. As they pulled up on the driveway, they tried not to look at the crime scene.

Wheatley suggested the boys take their sedative. In the kitchen, Fran broke a tablet in half, then heated some milk. He poured the warm, frothy liquid into two glasses, and handed it to the boys with their halves of the pill. They were quickly unconscious. 'It's your turn now,' Wheatley said. But Fran and Marie didn't want the tablet, as tempting as oblivion was, because to be unconscious was to forfeit the opportunity to be told the cops had got it wrong. It was to forsake the chance to will the news false with fervent prayer and incantation. To be unconscious — to *want* to be unconscious — was to concede the worst. And Wheatley knew this. She was familiar with grief's elaborate games of peek-a-boo. 'I'm not leaving until I've seen you take them,' she said.

Fran and Marie washed theirs down with brandy, and Wheatley left, telling them she'd be back first thing in the morning. The Ryles went to bed and fell asleep. At about three in the morning, Fran was startled from nothingness by screaming, and he found himself swimming in murky water, up towards the surface light of full consciousness. But once he broke the surface, it still seemed like a dream, a trick of the pill. Marie was beside the bed in her nightie, sobbing mightily and repeating the words *I'm gonna get my baby.*

The sedative may have been strong enough for a horse, but it wasn't strong enough to quell Marie's horror.

From the moment of ingestion, a wrestle began between chemical tranquillity and the belief that her daughter lay dead in the rain across the road. The wrestling continued in sleep, and horror was triumphant. Marie believed her daughter was still lying there. Alone and in the rain. But her body had been transferred to the morgue hours before.

Was Fran dreaming? He wasn't sure. If he was dreaming, he could stop trying to peer through the fog at the consequences of Marie reclaiming her daughter's body. But each time she said it — each time she said, 'I'm gonna get my baby' — the fog receded. And then she was gone. Fran had only made it to the front door by the time Marie was across the street. Here was the hysterical pilgrimage that Wheatley had feared.

There was an unmarked police car near their house, stationed to keep an eye on the crime scene. Three detectives were inside, chatting and drinking coffee. Seeing Marie dash across the park, they leapt out and tried to cut her off. Fran watched helplessly from the driveway as the large detectives — '6 foot 4 and built like prop forwards' — tried to stop her, but, powered by hysteria, she surged through them like a tugboat. She got close to the site before being subdued and brought to the car. She and Fran got in the back, and the detectives poured them coffees from their thermos.

Somehow they got back to sleep, waking at 8.00 am when the radio alarm came on. Harry Nilsson's 'Without You' suddenly filled the room. '*No, I can't forget this evening, or your face as you were leaving/But I guess that's just the way the story goes.'* Marie reached over and hurled the radio into the wall.

News spread quickly. Mindarie College wasn't far from the primary school, and on Thursday morning the place was electric with rumours. 'There was unrest at the school that day,' teacher Katy Warner remembered. 'There was a lot of discussion between students.'

'It was an odd feeling,' recalled a former student. 'A lot of whispering.'

Many students were concerned it was a peer of theirs, but when staff learnt the victim was 19, most assumed it couldn't have been one of their kids. But among pupils, Rebecca's name was mentioned in the anxious exchange of rumours. Katy Warner started her drama period — the one in which Rebecca was enrolled — and realised that most of her class believed Rebecca had been murdered. 'It's not Becky,' Warner told her class. 'It's definitely not.'

One student wasn't convinced by Warner's assurance, and became agitated. Warner asked if it would help if she called Rebecca's mum. 'I'll do it here, in front of you. And Becky's mum will tell us that she's just in bed sick today.' Warner never made the call.

Later that afternoon, while Warner was taking another class, the school psychologist came into the room. Warner immediately knew what this meant: it *was* Rebecca. The psych told Warner to go to the staff room, while she would stay with the students.

The staff were in shock. Many were crying. There was a sense of unreality. Many couldn't assimilate the knowledge. It was deeply, alarmingly, incongruous. 'We just couldn't believe it was happening,' said Warner. 'Could. Not. Believe.' The fact that Warner had told her class it wasn't Rebecca has long stayed with her. She felt early on that she had let them down, and apologised to them for it. 'I felt like I had let Becky down, too,' she said. 'I remember that on that Wednesday I could have asked her to come in to school. It was a day of extra study. I always wished I asked her to come in. You never know, it could have gone differently.'

Students were numb, nauseated, or recklessly livid. Groups of girls sobbed together. Groups of guys plotted vengeance against faceless enemies. Rebecca's friend Nathan was questioned by police, which fed the rumour mill. The school became a greenhouse of grief and speculation. 'When the Claremont serial killings happened,' Warner told me, 'there was always someone who knew someone who knew someone. People have this morbid sense of wanting to be connected in some way. And there was a lot of that going on, and it aggravated some students.'

It's likely the teachers were as affected as their students, but they didn't admit it. Katy Warner wasn't much older than Rebecca, and was devastated by her death, but she didn't seek any help. Warner felt selfish even contemplating it, when her job, as she described it, was to create a safe place for her students.

On the Friday morning, 24 hours after the discovery of Rebecca's body, the college held a whole-of-school assembly. The principal spoke, assuring pupils that help was at hand. They would get through this together. Additional counsellors were recruited. 'It was surreal,' a student told me. 'Groups of girls walking around the school crying. The male teachers trying to keep a stiff upper lip.'

Rebecca's brother, Chris, was in the same year. Because of what happened, and the subsequent time he took off, he repeated the year in 2005. He spent a lot of time in the library, which served both his intellectual curiosity and his desire for solitude. There were other problems when Chris returned to school. The younger brother of the man charged with Rebecca's murder had enrolled there, too. Teachers appealed to the principal to reject it, believing the enrolment would dishonour Rebecca and prove terribly disruptive to students, including the brother himself. But the application was approved.

THREE

BOYS WILL BE BOYS

James Duggan drank beer and smoked dope on the steps of the Clarkson Mini Mart. It's a small, drab shopping village on the suburban fringes, built out of the same pale bricks as his house. It comprises a tattoo parlour, liquor and grocery stores, and a fish-and-chip shop. Duggan pulled bongs and drank here with people, including my brother. Before they turned 18, before the group drifted apart, this is where they spent their time, between house parties and parents' patios.

James was rarely close to those he drank with. He was quiet, sour, and couldn't hold his booze, which embarrassed his assumed identity. Those who knew James often saw him sitting quietly, desperately trying to mask his drunkenness. It was crucial to him that he conceal it, but he was rarely successful. On many nights, the group, having decided to leave the steps for a party or a patio, would march off while James lingered drunkenly behind. He was trapped. He could neither drink more, nor be seen without a bottle in his hand. His solution was to secretly empty its contents as he lagged behind the others. But he was indiscreet. Everyone knew what he was doing.

It was all part of the obligatory front — a tireless performance enacted by many male teenagers occupying the space between adolescence and adulthood. And so, despite his slim physique, James affected the role of the hard man. One part of the role involved pretending to be better with booze than he actually was. Another was plotting drug scores or retaliatory beatings, or riffing crudely on the virtues of women.

Near the Mini Mart was a narrow laneway, which was closer still to an 'open house' — a place open to whoever wanted to score drugs. No reference was required here; strangers could roll up and buy. So the laneway became strategically prized by the more violently ambitious, and feared by those who weren't. It was the perfect place to beat a rival, or to strip someone of newly acquired gear. James once claimed he had been mugged in the laneway and roughly dispossessed; but, given his inclination to lies and exaggeration, his story was dismissed. His plots of vengeance were shelved.

Despite his fantasies of robbing rivals, James's thefts were weak and opportunistic. He stole money and drugs from those around him, triggering his social exile and an awkward embrace with another group. His social life was cyclical: he would burn a bridge by engaging in theft or dishonesty, move on, burn another, and then retreat across the previous bridge that had been delicately repaired in an act of convenience. Their social groups were largely fickle and porous, but by the end Gareth Phillips was one of his last remaining friends.

Duggan had once belonged to a tagging crew called OES. In this area, you'd see plenty of graffiti tags — furtive swirls of ego, ugly and hurriedly expressed. Members long debated what their acronym should definitively stand for. Some argued for 'On Every Street', as a reference to the supposed ubiquity of their tags and influence. Others preferred the cartoonish 'On Evil Substances'. Still others thought it should be '1-8-7', a US police code for homicide, and popularised by Dr. Dre's debut single 'Deep Cover'.

Typically, crews would express their names in three-letter acronyms. Ones I knew included IBS, or International Bombing Squad ('bombing' being synonymous with 'tagging'), and NRA, or No Respect for Authority. Competing with Duggan's crew was BF, or Black Fighters, a gang composed largely of Aboriginal kids and feared by many, including my brother.

In retrospect, the crew names seem analogous to the stage names of professional wrestlers. They're theatrical signifiers of villainy. Like the wrestlers, many simply inhabited a role. But unlike the wrestlers, who knew they were actors, some within the crews were capable of actual violence. Probably the better comparison is found in the culture that so much of the graffiti scene aped — US hip-hop. Individual rappers, like taggers, had their own *noms de guerre*. They were also associated with their aggressively named crews — bands, political affiliations, or record labels.

There were many writing tools available to the tagger. A rock might be used to engrave a bus window; a spray can to emblazon a wall or bus shelter. Perhaps the most popular were giant permanent markers — ones with a chiselled nib to better render the tag calligraphically. Vandals were not without aesthetic discernment. Pleasure could be found in bold and unhesitating lines, ones that contained a fluid transfer between thick and thin.

There were defacements of the defacements — an urban palimpsest. Crew members would routinely strike out suspect tags. This was called 'slashing', and a signature might be censured if (a) the tag was already in use, (b) it was judged to be stylistically meritless, or (c) there was a need to act vengefully against a rival gang or gang member. Option (b) supposed a proud and practised aesthetic, and after a while you could spot the 'toy' tags, the ones guilelessly incapable of emulating it.

While I never tagged, I developed a style on paper, and provided one of the area's more prolific vandals with his sobriquet. It was 'Bubster', but was more often used in its diminutive form of 'Bubsie'. The 's' could be substituted for a 'z', and this small degree of versatility helped commend it to my friend.

Bubsie was a giddy proponent of the crime. In high school, he was interested in little but drugs, football, and refining his craft. In class, he would fill notebooks with experimental iterations of his tag, which he offered to me for judgement. After I graduated from high school, I stopped seeing him, but I would still frequently spot his handiwork. I felt complicit, but I also knew he was inveterate. He would have used another tag had I never gifted him 'Bubsie'.

One day, perhaps six months into university, I spotted a copy of the *West Australian* at the train station's kiosk. Bubsie was on the front page. He was grinning shamelessly outside court, after a hearing on vandalism charges had collapsed into farce — and contempt — after his mates heckled the magistrate from the gallery. Presumably there was some apocalyptic hook for the story — the criminal malaise of our generation, perhaps. My father saw it, too. 'Wasn't he a mate of yours?' he asked. I conceded that he had been.

Norman Mailer once celebrated the audacity of the vandal. He admired the transgression. It was another chapter, he thought, in 'the long war of the will against the power of taboo'. It's a long bow. If Mailer's subjects were anything like the guys I knew, he was romanticising petty crudity. It was vulgar and destructive. True, some like Bubsie found satisfaction in refinement, attaching an admirable discipline to deeply anti-social instincts. And for a small minority, the thrill would later be developed into artistic pieces, assuredly social and skilful. But, for most of the crew members I knew, it was simple: tags were just another form of violence.

Still, you couldn't underestimate the power of glimpsing the streets as an endless canvas. Crews had two discrete audiences: the public, who were simply meant to be affronted; and their small underground of peers — both colleagues and rivals — upon whom would be impressed a sense of skill, risk, or territorial domination.

The Black Fighters, though, were more interested in asserting that domination through uncompromising violence. They were implicated in a number of deaths. At one trial for an unlawful killing, an Afghani taxi driver testified as a witness to the death of Leon Robinson on Christmas Eve 2002. Only 18 months later, he would drive James Duggan home on the night of Rebecca's murder.

My brother knew to be wary of Jeremiah Farmer and his BF boys. They were a spiteful pack, cruising the northern suburbs, crashing parties and dealing drugs. Even among thugs, they were renowned for their signatures of ultra-violence — baseball bats and knives.

On Christmas Eve 2002, cabbie Ajmal Azizi was driving down West Coast Highway along the coastline in Perth's northern suburbs. It was dark, and he was driving past Hillarys Boat Harbour, home of the Breakwater Tavern. A 20-year-old electrician, Leon Robinson, had been drinking there all afternoon with friends and his girlfriend. Drunk and impatient for a taxi, Leon and his mates began flagging random cars down from the highway. They picked the wrong one. A Commodore, driven by Farmer and filled with three other teenagers, pulled over. Words, then blows, were exchanged. Leon was struck to the ground, and repeatedly kicked. His girlfriend screamed for the attackers to stop. Jeremiah and his mates dragged Leon's unconscious body to the side of the road and sped off. Ajmal saw all this, as did a nurse who raced over to perform CPR on Leon. It wasn't enough. On Christmas morning, Leon died. A tear in his heart was discovered during the autopsy.

During the first trial of the four boys, which was ultimately aborted by the judge, Leon's girlfriend testified to seeing a 'big, chubby man with curly hair' punch Leon about four times and then 'smack' him to the ground, where he lay motionless. That chubby man was a boy then, and his name is Cameron Murcutt, aka Cam Merky. In 2012, the 'Boy from Balga' became a Western Australian kickboxing champion after he defeated Brad 'Redzone' Russell in Perth's eastern suburbs.

You can watch Murcutt's fight clips on YouTube. He competes in Muay Thai kickboxing and cage fighting, and his bouts have been broadcast on pay TV. He's recognisable from the photos taken of him scurrying from court when he was a teenager. He's still large, but he's not chubby anymore. He has a dull, piggish face and small eyes. These days he wears a rat's tail with short sides.

I watched his kickboxing contest against Steve Behan, then ranked 9th in the country. Murcutt, much shorter than his opponent, was nevertheless confident. He never hesitated. As soon as the bell rang, he unleashed his ferocity, knocking Behan out with a shuddering right. Behan slumped inelegantly on the ropes, while Murcutt jumped triumphantly around the ring. I was amazed. Murcutt hadn't run away from the instincts that had contributed to a man's death — he had studied, refined, then practised them professionally. The thug had turned pro. In an interview in 2012, Murcutt said, 'I never wanna give up, won't stop 'til I'm KO'd. It's my background — growing up in the Bronx of Perth taught me a lot. I fight because I meet good people. Self discipline, travel, get respect, test the boundaries.'

Murcutt escaped conviction for Robinson's killing — the four were eventually acquitted after a retrial could not determine the cause of death — but he was found guilty in 2006 of making threats before the manslaughter retrial the year before. Two witnesses to the beating of Leon Robinson — Harris Hajah-Mydin and his then partner Melanie Hopkins — were shopping at a mall in Mirrabooka, an economically depressed suburb in Perth's north. Murcutt, free on bail, bumped into them. 'Youse are all gonna die and your houses are going to get burnt down. Youse are dogs.' The chubby boy then moved right up into the face of Hajah-Mydin: 'You're a dog cunt.'

When I compare photos of Cameron Murcutt — overweight, goofy, but menacing — with recent shots of Cam Merky — naked from the waist up, silk shorts, gloves, and bruises — I see not so much a warrior as a man who desperately needs to think himself one. The Murcutt that emerges from the court reporting is a burgeoning crook and a dangerous child. Compare that with the photos taken of him at his gym, flexing his muscles in the centre of the shot, surrounded by coaches and protégés. He's someone now. Someone who loftily compares his upbringing to Jake LaMotta's in the Bronx. Someone who 'gets respect.'

Joel Robinson moved into his dead brother's house. It helped somehow.

FOUR
THE BOAT

Wednesday morning, 5 May 2004. It was four days after his 19th birthday, and James Duggan woke and lay in bed. It was 10.00 am. He was in no hurry. James was an unemployed high-school dropout. Six months prior, he had worked in a bakery; before that, he'd pushed trolleys at Ocean Keys shopping centre. James had been rostered on one New Year's Eve — a heavy day for trolley jockeys — but he never showed up. James's partner — my brother Howard — cursed his absence as he desperately pushed the long, mischievous snakes around the asphalt alone. Duggan never returned.

Duggan was scrawny, with a face dusted with bum fluff. He had short brown hair, closely cropped on the sides, and dutifully wore the teen uniform: skate and surf T-shirts, jeans and sneakers. He was boyishly handsome, with fine features. He was English, too, born in Liverpool in 1985, from where he watched his parents' divorce when he was young. James's mother, Michaela, was remarried to a Paul Duggan before they moved to Australia in 1996, and James took his name and called him 'Dad'. But in 2000 they split, too, and Paul found his own place just a few kilometres away to make the joint custody of James's two half-brothers easier. They would continue to attend school at Mindarie Primary.

The divorce troubled James, but he wouldn't — or couldn't — verbalise it. Mindarie's dunes are thick with young masculine inarticulateness. James was moody and taciturn, but he did try a reunion with his biological father in England. He flew 15,000 kilometres, but it didn't go well. Within six months, James was flying back home, to live among the limestone and boredom. There was no girlfriend. Word was, James was weird around girls.

On this Wednesday, James woke in the house he shared with his mother and his friend Gareth. The three of them lived in Quinns Rocks, the suburb adjoining Mindarie to the north, in a compact two-storey. The house proper sat on the first storey above a double garage and Gareth's room. Stairs led from the concrete driveway on the ground floor to the front door on the first. The house was set back from a quiet street and stood nakedly, unprotected by any fence or hedge. To the right of the long driveway stood a tall palm tree, rising from buffalo grass. The bricks were beige; the roller-doors, cream. It was a mildly depressing house, brutally stark, but just over the hill and down the road lay the Indian Ocean.

That morning, like most mornings, James had 27 View Terrace to himself. Both Michaela and Gareth were working. His mother was employed at the Director of Public Prosecutions as a receptionist; Gareth was out pouring slabs of concrete at construction sites. Gareth made his money like many up there: using struts, tiles, concrete, or render to claim the dunes for others. To flourish in the Perth idyll often meant physically building it for others. He didn't see it that way, of course. It was just a job. He poured concrete. It meant early rises, early finishes, and more money than he had ever had in high school. With no rent to pay, there was plenty of cash for drinking.

Gareth had been kicked out of home, and Michaela agreed to accept him rent-free. He'd been living at View Terrace for about five months, and had known James for almost four years, from Clarkson High School. On weekends, Gareth played semi-professional soccer for Joondalup City. He worked hard, and played hard.

James used his freedom to channel surf, play Xbox, and watch a DVD — Kevin Smith's 2001 film *Jay and Silent Bob Strike Back,* a sort of Gen X re-boot of Cheech and Chong's woozy adventures. In 1994, inspired by Richard Linklater's cult classic *Slackers*, Smith shot a film for just $27,000, using the convenience and video stores he worked in as sets. He wrote, directed, and starred in it, and the film exploded. *Clerks* was Tarantino without any guns or plot. Enticingly articulate dropouts riffed pleasurably on pop culture and sex while taking a wry pride in their lack of ambition. The film was irreverent

and profane, and introduced characters that had rarely
been seen before. Its success no doubt had something
to do with the sharpness of the dialogue, but also the
brashness of the conceit: an assemblage of the nerdy and
unemployable, aimlessly playing out their day. Smith had
beatified stoners.

In 2001, Smith released a sequel of sorts, though this
time the budget was millions of dollars. Hollywood stars
were cast. Jay and Silent Bob must hitchhike, broke,
across the country from New Jersey to Hollywood to
sabotage a film being made about them. It is not so much
a plot as an excuse for Smith to wheel his two characters
into absurd situations.

Here was James Duggan, an unemployed pot smoker,
watching drug-obsessed slackers journey farcically across
the States. Was he laughing at them — or *with* them?
In an adoring review in *Rolling Stone*, Peter Travers
addressed the controversy generated by the film's surfeit
of gay jokes ('You eat the cock?'). Travers wrote: 'Smith's
argument for such jokes is that he wants to "preach
tolerance by hiding it with humour". What's sad is that
Smith has to keep justifying his right to parody prejudice
and skewer male adolescents.'

But it's doubtful that most male adolescents know it.
I'd wager that they see it as an endorsement, not a droll
condemnation. James Duggan was laughing *with* them.
Which is not to say the film or jokes shouldn't be made,
but how teenage boys interpret art and entertainment
can deviate wildly from the maker's intent.

Growing up on this coastal strip, I saw this slippage all the time. The political passion behind some music became a mirror for the apolitical tumult within its teenage listener — the ordinary mess of hormones and an unfinished frontal cortex. Any nuanced ambition the artist might have for the song was engulfed by his listener's narcissism. The progressive brimstone of Rage Against the Machine became anthems for thugs. A Metallica song about religious excess would be shorn of everything but its contempt, and become an endorsement of violence. Cypress Hill's humour and winking mischief was ignored. For me, this music was the backdrop to groped girls, cracked skulls, flashed knives, and police sirens. Rage Against the Machine may have wanted revolution, but they were unwittingly sound-tracking destruction in suburbs all over the Western world.

James Duggan sat on his couch and laughed.

Gareth got home from work around three o'clock that afternoon, and cracked open a six-pack of VB with James. Gareth had already drunk two stubbies of Coopers before getting home. Now he polished off two more of the Bitter. He was getting loose. At about 4.00, Gareth called his brother Sam and asked if he wanted to go to The Boat later. Sam said yes — he could come for a little bit, and he and his girlfriend would pick Gareth up at 5.30.

The Boat was boisterous on Wednesdays. It was the night to be there. Senior high schoolers would try to sneak in among the Brits and young tradies. Wednesday was also the night for Chase the Ace, a popular game of chance. Every drink you bought got you a raffle ticket. If your number was called, you walked up to the host, who fanned a pack of cards before you. If you picked the ace of spades, you won cash. If you didn't, you got a Jim Beam beanie. Your odds were low, but that's what made it fun.

Sam and Nicole could see James and Gareth standing at the front of the house as they parked in the driveway. Gareth wore a blue shirt, jeans, and skate shoes; James, a white T-shirt, grey surf jacket, jeans, and sneakers. Gareth walked to the car window and asked them if it was okay if his friend James came along. 'No worries,' Sam said, and the four of them drove down to the pub. They found a table outside on the water.

James and Gareth were just getting started. Gareth bought a pint of VB; James got himself a jug. Normally reserved for communal drinking, the solo jug was common among James's friends, and a macho signature of a serious drinker. Sam and Nicole didn't stay long. At 7.00, they left so Nicole could call her son and get home in time for her favourite TV show, *McLeod's Daughters*. James and Gareth were drunk when they farewelled the two, but they would get drunker. Sam and Nicole would later testify that James and Gareth were just 'merry' when they left.

James and Gareth now moved inside. They knew others there; they always knew others there. There was Nathan sitting up at a table by the fireplace, and with him was Iain — respectively, a roof tiler and a musician. They talked nonsense for half an hour or so, and Nathan and Iain noticed James's and Gareth's speech becoming increasingly slurred. Nathan went to the bar, and saw his friend Rebecca Ryle enter.

'Hiya, Nathan.'

'Hey.'

'How was your day?'

Rebecca ordered a beer; Nathan bought a Bundy and Coke. The two moved back to the table up by the fireplace, and Nathan introduced Rebecca to James and Gareth.

What followed was loose conversation, haltingly engaged in by the two drunks. Rebecca was sober and spirited, smoking cigarettes and nursing her beer. James and Gareth knew others there from Clarkson High School — Adam, Gary, and Brett. The three of them didn't intend to stay long, just until Chase the Ace was drawn at 9.00, and then they were off to a friend's birthday at a nearby marina. James got wind of the fact that they would soon be driving to Bar 120 at Hillarys Boat Harbour, and asked if he could join them. Gary had to figure out how to tell him 'no' — James was already rowdy and obnoxious, slurring vulgarities at passing strangers. At 9.20, the three of them — Adam, Gary, and Brett — drove down the coast to Hillarys to keep drinking. They had managed to avoid taking James.

Iain and Nathan were the next to leave, at 10.20. Iain had driven Nathan down, and had promised to drive him back. Before he left, he asked Rebecca if she wanted a lift. 'No, thanks,' she said. Nathan gave her a hug goodbye.

James returned to the table, where he lit a Peter Jackson and knocked back more beer. It was nearly the eleven o'clock closing time, but there were still plenty of people around. Gareth had a wild look in his eye. He went down to the bar to get more booze, and found an unattended mobile phone. He slipped it under the elastic strap of his boxer shorts, but he made two mistakes: one was drunkenly bringing attention to his act; the second was choosing a large Maori man's phone to swipe. Suddenly, Gareth had two large blokes — John and Jacob — laying into him. From where they sat, up near the fireplace, Rebecca and James could only see a confused mass of bodies. There was plenty of shouting.

Vicki, the bar manager, rushed into the fray and tried to separate them, before Andrew the bouncer arrived and escorted John and Jacob out the front entrance that leads onto the car park. Vicki turned her attention to Gareth, asking him for some ID. 'It'll be much simpler this way,' she said to him, and Gareth took out his wallet and began handing over his licence. Vicki reached for it, but Gareth had a sudden change of heart, shoving her and sprinting off out the back. His friends watched as another Maori man — an off-duty bartender called Nuds — dashed out the back entrance after Gareth. Andrew caught up with him, too. In her statement to police, made the following month, Vicki would write of Gareth: 'In the last six months I have probably seen him no more than three times. He has a bit of a cocky attitude and speaks with an Australian accent.'

'Fuck off! Get the fuck off me!' Gareth screamed, and he took a swing at Andrew. He missed, and was quickly placed in a headlock while he thrashed around. John and Jacob had, by this point, been convinced to leave the area while the bar manager called the police. Andrew and Nuds were now trying to calm Gareth down, sitting him on a limestone wall, and promising to release him from the grip if he calmed down.

'Let me go, and I'll just wait here with you for the police,' Gareth said.

They loosened their grip. Gareth bolted.

'Run, Forrest, run!' someone yelled — it was a clichéd reference to the film *Forrest Gump* — as Gareth fled from security up through the car park. As was the style, his skate shoes were not properly tied, the laces merely tucked inside the shoe. Within metres, his right shoe fell off onto the asphalt. He kept running.

As Gareth jogged through the dunes, the bar closed, and a few people milled about on the boardwalk. Two of them were James and Rebecca. The police had been called, and would arrive shortly. James was holding the right Rip Curl sneaker as Vicki approached him. 'What's your friend's name?' she asked.

'Liam,' he lied.

'Liam what?'

'Liam Holmes.'

'Do you know where he lives?'

'Limetree Circuit.'

'That's just behind the primary school, isn't it?'

'Yeah.'

James had given Vicki a false name — but not an invented one. Liam Holmes existed, and he lived where James said he did. Liam was a friend, or an ex-friend, of James's.

And then the security camera, fixed to the front of The Boat, captured James and Rebecca walking away through the car park.

And it captured them coming back. Rebecca needed the bathroom, and began knocking on the glass doors. A Boat regular who knew Rebecca slightly — and had seen the earlier fracas with Gareth — jokingly said to her, 'You're not gonna get served!'

Rebecca laughed. 'Oh, I know. I just need to use the bathroom.'

Ryan, a bartender, came to the door and told her that he couldn't let her in, but seeing police pull up into the car park, he thought he might as well — it was safe with them there, and he'd have to unlock the door for them anyway. Rebecca thanked him, and dashed to the toilet. James waited outside. It was 11.25 pm.

'You'd want to be more careful about who your friends are, mate,' a patron said to James. He had watched it all unfold, and had taken James to be a placid kid with bad friends. James exploded: 'You have a fucking problem?!'

'No, mate. No.'

'What the fuck are you saying, then?'

The man mumbled some apologies and made a hasty retreat to his car. At this moment, both the police and Rebecca were inside. As Rebecca left the bathroom, she saw Eden, the girlfriend of the bartender who let her in, sitting at a table. 'I just hate going to the toilet in the bushes,' Rebecca laughed. 'I'll just hold on for ages if I have to.'

'Me too,' Eden agreed.

Rebecca was relaxed and cheerful. She said goodnight to Eden, and went back outside to James.

The police departed soon after, at 11.35, followed by Ryan and Eden.

It was just Vicki left now. She counted the tills, secured the cash in the safe, and then ensured that each window and door was properly bolted. As she checked the windows that overlooked the marina's boat pens, she saw three figures on a grassy patch near an apartment development. It was dark, nearing midnight, and the figures were 300 metres away, but she was sure they were James, Gareth, and Rebecca — and she said so in a statement. But in time the memory faded, and became less trustworthy.

As James and Rebecca left The Boat and walked again across the car park, they were leaving the gaze of witnesses and cameras. Rebecca was falling off the grid. Ninety minutes later, James would re-enter the frame of verifiable movement when he walked into a petrol station, and CCTV and a service attendant could resume the story. But those crucial 90 minutes would remain frustratingly opaque to investigators, though pleasingly accommodating of the defence's alternative theories. Nature may abhor a vacuum, but defence lawyers love one.

The time between 11.30 pm and 1.00 am remains mysterious. But here is what we know: we know that James and Rebecca walked up Honiara Way with their backs to the ocean, and that streetlamps and pine trees lined the street. We know that Honiara Way climbs steeply towards the park, away from the beach, and that the front walls of most of the homes are made of limestone. We know that as they walked they found Gareth's second shoe, and that James picked it up and made a pair.

We know that James was drunk and Rebecca sober, and the streets were quiet. We know that as they crossed Rothesay and came to the park, Rebecca's house was just 100 metres away. We know that both were born beyond the inky horizon behind them, and that James had lost his native accent, but that Rebecca, here only six months, had kept hers. We know that Rebecca was carrying her black handbag.

We know that they walked through streets that were rich with fearlessness and filled with sleeping children whose school would be shut when they woke. We know that James told police that they sat on the wooden bollards that ring the oval, and each removed one of their cigarettes and lit it. We know that James smoked Peter Jacksons. We know that James told police that they kissed, and we know that James pinned Rebecca in a headlock and strangled her to death. We know that to kill someone in this way requires sustained pressure for at least three minutes. We know that James later said of the moment he was choking Rebecca that 'everything was spinning around', and we know that Fran, Marie, Chris, and Andrew were sleeping just across the street as James was spinning out of orbit.

We know that while Rebecca was in this death-hold, a delicate galaxy of capillaries was rupturing in her neck. We know that her nose bled, and that the filthy sleeve of James's jacket was stained by it. We know that James told police that she did not struggle, that she went limp quickly and then slumped to the ground. We know that when Peter Carter and his blue heeler discovered Rebecca roughly seven hours later, her pants were flung on a classroom roof and her pink underwear had been removed and left beside her. We know that a part of her cardigan was missing, that her bra was twisted, and that the contents of her handbag were scattered nearby.

James ran. He did not call for help on his phone, or bang on the doors of neighbours. He ran. But before he did so, he collected Gareth's shoes, Rebecca's phone, and the earrings in her handbag. Then he ran past Rebecca's house to Limetree Circuit, where James's father and brothers were sleeping, and dumped Rebecca's Nokia down a drain in front of number seven. Then he kept running in his bloodstained jacket to the Mobil Quix petrol station a couple of hundred metres away.

Luke Richards had been working the graveyard shift at Mobil Mindarie for six months, three days a week, from 11.00 pm to 7.00 am. In the afternoons, he worked in a bottle shop. It was a brutal regime, and he despised it, but he'd saved enough to travel. He was just two weeks away from finishing; two weeks away from escaping overseas. Luke was 20, a year older than James and Rebecca, and by the time James came in at 12.55 am he'd already had enough. It was always the same — a medley of meth heads, young drunks, and younger thieves. That night, Luke had already served a guy who'd smoked a rock at home, and had come in for cigarettes and conversation. Then there were the young shits who lifted hot pies and legged it. Around midnight, the car park was filled with teenage drunks blasting music from their vehicles. Luke called the cops. It was a regular Wednesday night at the servo.

So when James walked in, holding Gareth's shoes and slurring, he was far from the most memorable or threatening person Luke had seen that night. The previous two hours had already cast Luke as the ineffectual master of a circus, and he was playing it cool. *Don't escalate anything*, he told himself, *and in two weeks you'll be gone, screaming towards Europe at 35,000 feet*.

'You got a number for a taxi?' James slurred. Luke was unforgiving in his judgement of James — he was another idiot conscripted to torment him — but he politely gave him the number. Before James walked to the payphone, he asked for some change.

Luke had a simple strategy for drunks: don't insult their intelligence, and don't engage them beyond what is absolutely necessary. Luke handed over some shrapnel, and James made his way over to the phone, pouring the silver into the narrow slot. Then he punched some numbers, very likely the wrong ones.

'It's not working, it's not working,' James said, but Luke knew very well that it was.

'Can you call the cab for me?' James asked.

'What's your name?'

'James Duggan.'

'Where you going?'

'Quinns Rocks.'

Luke booked the cab, and was told the wait was upwards of an hour. He didn't like the idea of hosting James for that long, but that's how it went on the graveyard shift.

James walked up to the counter. 'What's it like working here?'

Luke shrugged. 'It's just a job.'

'Went down to The Boat tonight for my birthday,' James said. 'My mate got into a fight and then got chased by the bouncer and he lost his shoes, but we found them,' he said, indicating the sneakers.

Luke was bored, but far from intimidated. He was cursing his luck that another 'drunk, uneducated dickhead' was fucking with his night, and wished fervently for the arrival of the cab. He didn't notice the bloodstain on the right sleeve, and didn't notice that when James wandered outside to dump the jacket and earrings in a skip bin behind the station, he came back into the store wearing only a T-shirt.

James pulled a sandwich and a drink from the fridge, and took them to the counter. He paid, and Luke bagged the items with Gareth's pair of shoes. James wandered over to the window and looked out. Luke thought he saw a cab approaching. 'I think your taxi's coming,' he said, but then realised his error. 'Oh, it's just a police car.'

'There's a lot of police around tonight,' James mumbled, and walked over to the magazine rack, selecting *Picture* — a three-dollar soft porno mag — and took it to the counter. Luke stuffed it in the same bag with the drink and sandwich. 'Why don't you just walk home?' Luke asked.

James answered that he was too tired and that he wouldn't be able to get up for work in the morning if he did. Luke sighed. James wandered back outside.

When he came back in, he walked to the counter and pointed to the M&M figurines on display behind Luke. They were 'Motor Mates' — dashboard ornaments with suction-cap feet. 'I want to buy those.' They went into the bag, too, and James leant on the counter. He'd been hanging around for nearly 40 minutes now, and Luke thought he was more sober. Luke could not know that James had neither a job nor a car.

About 1.40 am, Swan taxi #581, driven by Ajmal

Azizi, arrived. James said goodbye, and Luke went back to cleaning the hotdog stand. Later, when Azizi was called to testify at the murder trial, he would think it strange that it was his second time in two years as a witness to an unlawful killing. Stranger still that it had happened in Western Australia, so far from his hometown of Jalalabad in eastern Afghanistan.

James got into the front passenger seat of the cab. He appeared to Ajmal as a 'young boy, normal and happy.' He had his bag of drink, food, porn, shoes, and figurines.

'How's your night been?' James asked.

'It's been very quiet. It's Wednesday.'

James didn't seem drunk to Ajmal, and his passenger directed him to View Terrace. It was a very short trip — five minutes at most — and James paid and left. Ajmal thought nothing of him.

Before James got home just before 2.00 am, Gareth had woken Michaela when he fumbled with the lock on his door. Michaela's bedroom was directly above Gareth's, and she got up and came out to the balcony to peer down and inspect the source of the noise. She saw Gareth shoeless, 'shaking and nervous'. He was also obviously drunk.

'Do you know where James is?' she asked.

'No, probably still at The Boat,' he replied.

James's mother wasn't exactly sure what time this conversation took place. She testified to seeing a '1, 2, and a 6' on the digital-clock display, but that could've meant anything — 11.26, 12.16, 1.26 — and that's assuming she recalled the jumble of numbers correctly. Regardless, Michaela put Gareth's arrival home at just 20 minutes before James, which is strange given he had fled The Boat almost three hours previously. Gareth later argued to police that if James had gotten home around 2.00, then he'd preceded him by a lot — that 11.26 would be the more likely arrangement of numbers.

Before James walked up the stairs to the front door, he placed Gareth's shoes at his friend's door. Then he let himself in. His mother woke again, and heard her son going to the fridge, the bathroom, and then, finally, to bed. She went back to sleep.

Rebecca's body had been found by the time James woke up. When he did, he was alone. Gareth, hungover, was pouring slabs in the nearby suburb of Butler. Before he left the house that morning, at around 7.00, Gareth noticed his shoes outside his door, and brought them inside. Between 9.00 and 10.00 am, Gareth returned home between jobs to get something to eat. James was up.

'Hey.'

'Man, what happened last night?' Gareth asked.

'You stole this Maori guy's phone and then he punched you, and the bouncers got you, but you ran away.'

'What about my shoes?'

'They fell off when you ran. They'd called the police, man.'

'Fuck.'

When Gareth asked Duggan what had happened the previous night, I speculate it was with a sense of pride. He knew he had made a stir, and the amnesiac effects of the booze likely glamourised his provocations. Behaviours that would probably induce shame today were signatures of pride back then. As teenagers, that's what action and influence looked like. Immaturity boiled these things down to anti-social disruption, so far away did real and constructive influence seem. For most, jobs and children would eventually replace delinquency. For most, all of the armour and apparatus of egos — skate clothes, binge drinking, aerosol cans, tiny notoriety, fists, cocks, cars — might come to seem pathetically inadequate.

Gareth ate something, then left.

Michaela was at work, too, when she received a call from a colleague about the murder. Apparently it was on the radio.

'Don't your sons go to Mindarie Primary School?'

'Yes,' Michaela said, and she hung up and called James.

'I want you to go over to your father's place and look after the boys. The school's closed today because a young girl's been found there.'

This was it. Confirmation, if he needed it, that Rebecca was dead. He felt nothing — neither sad nor happy. He hung up and made his way over to his stepdad's place to babysit his brothers. Gareth had also heard the news, from a radio at the construction site. 'A 19-year-old woman was found ...' The story was played on the hour each hour during the newsbreak. Gareth didn't think much of it.

James spent the day at his stepdad's keeping an eye on his two younger brothers, Michael and Matt. Their dad came home a little before 5.00 pm and drove them to rugby practice. James waited for his mum to pick him up before they drove home together. Gareth was already there. He'd finished work that day at 1.00, and had come home and slept until 4.30. Gareth asked James if they knew the girl.

'Nah, I don't think so.'

Gareth wanted to talk about it. James didn't. It was likely the last conversation they ever had with each other.

While Gareth was pouring concrete, while Michaela was answering phones in the office of the Director of Public Prosecutions, and while James babysat across the road from the crime scene, investigators were combing the place where Rebecca had last been seen alive: The Boat. CCTV gave them an image of her walking away with a young man; numerous witnesses gave them a name. Just after 11.00 that night, on Thursday 6 May, homicide detectives knocked on the door of 27 View Terrace with arrest warrants for James and Gareth. Michaela may have wondered who was knocking on her door that time of night. James probably didn't. The two young men were put into unmarked cars, and driven to the Joondalup police complex.

The Ryles were consumed by grief, and for a long while it became difficult to distinguish the days. They drank a lot. But for all the blurriness of that time, a few moments stand out. Perhaps the worst was visiting their daughter at the morgue.

Rebecca lay on an examiner's table, and Fran and Marie stared at her through a window. Fran stood quietly, feeling sick. Marie was sobbing and pawing the window, repeating, 'What's he done to you! What's he done to my baby?' A detective came over with a form. There were tears in his eyes, too. 'Do you recognise the deceased?' he asked, and he handed them the form. There was a section titled 'Relationship to the deceased.' With shaking hands, Fran wrote 'parents'.

The post-mortem hadn't been conducted yet, nor had Rebecca's body been cleaned. Her eyes were bulging slightly, and there was dried blood around her nose. 'This is barbaric,' Fran thought as he stared at his child. 'I can't forgive this. I can't move on.'

After the post-mortem, Marie asked Detective Wheatley if they could have the body back. Wheatley paused, before changing the topic. Marie repeated herself.

'Can we have her back now?'

There was another pause. 'You can, but she won't be complete.'

'What do you mean?'

Wheatley waited even longer this time before responding. 'She won't have a brain.'

Years later, Fran would say of that moment: 'There's some things that stick in your mind, things that you'll never erase. It's not a videotape where you can just delete the distasteful parts. The moment I'll never forget is when we had to go and identify Rebecca in the morgue. It was the most harrowing thing I've ever done in my life.

I've seen dead people before, but it was just grisly.

'There's a part of the judicial process, gathering evidence — the post-mortems — which is unpleasant, to say the least. What's going to happen to your daughter there? The pathologists do what they have to do, and your lovely daughter is reduced to a laboratory experiment. It's beyond the pale. I'm lost for words. I try to think about it, try to rationalise it, and *nothing*.'

Fran would remember the testimony of Dr Gerard Cadden, the forensic pathologist who examined his daughter. 'Yes, the brain was examined. The brain showed obvious congestive change. The brain was examined by two specialist neuropathologists, as was part of the spinal structures, and in respect to the brain the finding was congestion.'

And: 'In looking at the body undressed, the striking feature was the appearances at the head and neck level. The appearances of those regions of the body were in sharp contrast to the rest of the body … The colouration was different and the changes in respect to congestive changes of petechiae — those appearances were in sharp contrast to the rest of the body. By congestion, I am indicating that there has been a marked pooling of fluid in the head and neck, that blood has been trapped.'

In the Joondalup police centre, James was a boy trapped in the eye of a storm. Around him, the detectives quietly arrayed their talents. In that tiny interviewing room, with its bare white walls, round white table, and natty carpet, James was invisibly surrounded by techniques and reserves of patience much greater than his.

James sat meekly, his hands clasped and his head slightly bowed. Before him was a can of Coke, its colour matching his baggy red T-shirt. He rarely made eye contact. Before James sat Detective Sergeant Darren Bethell and Detective Sergeant Terence Rakich. They wore shirts and ties. They were relaxed. Gently, they read him his rights, and confirmed that he understood them. A verbal response was required; a begrudging one was given. It was 36 minutes before midnight.

It is usual — or it was in 2004 — for two detectives to sit in on an interview, though normally just one will lead. The other takes notes. Bethell led, and he began by asking Duggan his particulars.

'James, can you confirm your date of birth for us, please?'

'It's the first of the fifth, 1985.'

Rakich had his head lowered over his notepad, scribbling.

'Thank you. And were you born in Australia?'

'No, I was born in Liverpool, England. I've lived in Australia since 1996.'

James was speaking slowly, softly. He kept his eyes on the table before him.

'Okay, thank you. And can you tell me if you're currently working?'

'Um, no. I'm on Centrelink Youth Allowance.'

'Okay.'

If not rapport, an atmosphere of politeness was established. The dynamic of the interview had not yet risen above a meeting with a bank manager. But in time it would.

'Can you walk us through your previous 24 hours? From the moment you woke up yesterday.'

'No worries. I woke up about 10.00, then just stayed in the house. I was picked up by Gareth's brother's girlfriend at about 6.00. Had some drinks, then got a cab home. Before that, though, I stopped at Mobil and bought some chips and a magazine, and then I went to bed.'

'Okay, let's go back. When you woke, were you alone in the house?'

'Yes. Gareth and my mum work.'

'How do you know Gareth?'

'From school. He was kicked out of home and he was, like, staying with us in the room downstairs.'

'Okay. So, you got up at 10.00, and then what did you do?'

'I, like, watched a movie and played Xbox.'

'What movie did you watch?'

'It was *Jay and Silent Bob Strike Back*.'

'Okay.'

It is standard technique to quietly provide the suspect with a proverbial rope and allow him to hang himself with contradictions. In police interviews, this almost always starts with a variation on the following question: 'Tell us everything you can about your previous 24 hours. Don't leave anything out.' Undergirding this technique is the tenet 'Investigate, then interview. Don't interview, then investigate.' Eight years later, when Jill Meagher's killer, Adrian Bayley, was first interviewed by Victorian homicide detectives, the conversation began this way: 'Tell me everything from when you got home from work until you went to bed.' Bayley's was a nauseatingly confident and loquacious response. James's was timid, unsure.

In the light of James's reticence, Bethell was politely asking him to revisit those 24 hours, expanding upon what he had given them. James began to fill in the detail — the colour of his clothes, the money in his wallet, the types and quantity of beer he drank, who he saw there and what he said. Little by little, James began to create a detailed picture of the night.

As someone lying about One Big Thing, James appeared to relish telling the truth about the small stuff. He relished the appearance of credibility, the pretence of helpfulness. No detail was too small for him to furnish, and the sub-text was clear: *I'm here to help, detectives — whatever you need.* One could also imagine the temporary shelter that those tiny truths were creating to keep James from the much larger and incomprehensible truth that he had murdered Rebecca. Recalling what colour piping you had on your shoes is a slight but welcome distraction from the question of why you killed a stranger. You could slip inside the trivia, give yourself to it, block out everything but your earnest recollection of small facts that the detectives felt were so important. You could even feel useful. But those tiny shelters were hopelessly inadequate. They couldn't reverse the irreversible.

The restraint of the detectives so far was dutiful, but no less remarkable. They were certain they were sitting before a killer and a liar, one who was subtly revelling in his provision of prosaic detail. It would be grotesquely jarring for most of us, but this is what control looks like. Emotion can't exist. It's the enemy of a conviction.

'After Gareth's brother and his girlfriend left, what did you do then?'

'We went inside. We were sitting outside, then we went in. We knew people there.'

'Who did you know inside?'

'Adam and Gary and Brett.'

Detective Bethell's tone was still calm, reassuring. He asked for their full names, and their conversations.

'And that's when you met Rebecca?'

'I think so, yeah.'

'How long did you speak to Rebecca for?'

'About 10 minutes, around 11.00.'

'Only 10 minutes?'

'Yeah.'

'What did you talk about?'

'I don't remember.'

The gentleness that had been so consistent would soon be withdrawn, and Detective Rakich would finally break his silence.

'You say only 10 minutes, but we have witnesses saying you were talking to each other for a lot longer than that, James. And then we have you on tape leaving the premises with Rebecca. Can you explain this?'

'I, I, I don't know.'

'You were in her company for at least an hour and a half, weren't you?'

'I don't remember.'

'James, you left with Rebecca at about 11.30 and you didn't get home until 2.00, according to the taxi company. All of that time is unaccounted for.'

'I don't remember.'

This is where the apparently harmless invitation to volunteer small details was revealed as a trap. Depending on James's truthfulness, which depended upon how close he was in the chronology to the murder, he was either lucid or an amnesiac. By his own admission, he could recall everything in fine detail right up until the moment he sat beside Rebecca in the pub.

'You don't remember?'

'No.'

'But James, you remember everything else.' Rakich had him there. In the emotional arc of this interview, Rakich's dramatic inclusion elevated the sense of danger to James. Suddenly there were two of them, and the inquisitorial questions reinforced the threat. The pressure ratcheted up.

'James, you say you were only in Rebecca's company for ten minutes, but we know you were with her after that time. Can you explain that?'

'I'm not sure.'

'You're not sure?'

'I think she said she was going home, and she left.'

'You didn't leave with her?'

'No.'

'Aren't you a gentleman? You just left this girl to walk home alone?'

It was interesting bait, but James didn't take it. He was too weak, too guileless, to detect or respond to this impugning of his character. Or perhaps the rotten irony of the question turned his stomach. James knew that he *had* walked her home, but not because he was a gentleman.

The detectives continued to put specific times to him — when they knew he was with her, when they knew he had left with her. Nothing added up. James insisted that he hadn't left with her, that he had caught a cab from The Boat at 12.30. But between 11.00 and the professed 12.30 departure lay a vacuum. In the face of these questions, James's demeanour never really changed. He was a boy *and* a killer, mouthing weak recitations of innocence. As his words were batted back, he seemed to grow smaller.

'Did you touch Rebecca last night?'

'No.'

'James, you're getting yourself in a real tangle with us. Something went wrong last night. You know it and I know it, that's why you're here.'

The pressure increased again, the cards slowly placed upon the table. It was nearly 1.30 in the morning, and the period of patience was over. The detectives were now tangling him with his own contradictions; piercing him with his selective forgetfulness. Those invisible things that surrounded James when he first sat down were now revealing themselves. It had taken almost two hours, but the detectives' controlled momentum had reached its peak.

'I think you or Gareth or both of you walked Rebecca to the park. You wanted sex. She backed away, she made noise. You had to shut her up.'

James was shaking his head. 'No, no.'

'I want to find out about that hour and a half. I think you or you and Gareth took her to Mindarie Primary School. Things got out of hand and now she is dead. I'd like to see some remorse from you while we talk about this instead of all your denials. This is not going away. You've got yourself involved in something big, young man.'

James was insistent. 'I was not at Mindarie Primary School.'

Interviews would not — or should not — be conducted like this anymore. In Western Australia, this kind of accusatory, hypothetically charged argument has been scrapped. Interviews must be distinct from interrogations. Control is to be exercised subtly. Interviews should no longer possess the dramatic escalations of this one. At least, that is, if the participating investigators can control themselves. The reason for these changes is Dante Arthurs.

In 2006, eight-year-old Sofia Rodriguez-Urrutia Shu was shopping with her brother and uncle at a mall in Perth's southern suburbs. Arthurs was a 22-year-old trolley pusher there. He spotted Sofia alone, dragged her into the toilets, and raped and murdered her. 'The girl has got some shocking injuries,' the WA police commissioner said. 'It's a very disturbing crime. It's one of the worst that I've seen.'

Four years earlier, Arthurs had been charged with the sexual assault of another girl, but the charges were dropped after a pivotal police interview was considered too aggressive to be admissible in court. Arthurs walked. Years later, when he was arrested for the murder of Sofia, the WA police felt the wrath of the public. Talkback radio and editorials were unforgiving: if it weren't for police zealousness, Sofia would still be alive.

Staggeringly, the WA police did it again. In 2006, the Supreme Court of Western Australia dismissed the police interview with Arthurs about Sofia's murder because it had exceeded 'acceptable boundaries'. Charges of wilful murder were subsequently dropped, and Arthurs pleaded guilty to the lesser charge of murder and sexual assault. Despite the downgrade in charge, Arthurs was sentenced to life imprisonment, sparing the police further embarrassment.

It's not just for this reason that police interviews are important. The glossy fantasies of televised crime drama conceal the fact that the majority of criminal investigations are solved not with scientific evidence, but by clues obtained through interviews with suspects and witnesses. Because of this, investigative interviewing has become increasingly sophisticated, drawing its cues from behavioural psychology. This might run contrary to stereotypes of aggrieved detectives conducting 'robust' interviews — as was the case with Dante Arthurs — but, these days, investigators are trained to be 'open, interested, approachable, and personable'. It mightn't need years of research to tell you this, but this approach increases the chances of cooperation.

The interview with Adrian Bayley remains a textbook example. Bayley's sole interlocutor was unfailingly courteous, listened intently, and rarely interrupted. Eventually, contradictory elements were raised with Bayley, but they were introduced politely, almost as a point of curiosity rather than accusation. The detective — and the team behind him — had meticulously observed the four core skills of investigative interviewing: preparation, rapport, active listening, and intelligent questioning.

The art of investigative interviewing is also about negotiating the fragility of memory. To read a detective's handbook on memory is to imagine investigators as soldiers walking through a minefield, or doctors performing delicate surgery.

Memory is constantly under siege from trauma, stereotypes, suggestion, or partisanship. Our perceived reality is reconstructive, and alarmingly yoked to our likes and dislikes. Our memories are impure and unstable, and the very act of retrieval changes them. A famous study of this comes from 1974, and is included in Australian detective manuals. Called the 'Broken Glass' experiment, researchers Loftus and Palmer sought to prove that memories weren't factual recordings, but were inherently corruptible. In their research, the authors examined the influence of language on memory.

In their first experiment, subjects watched seven short clips of car accidents lifted from safety videos. They were then asked to answer questions about what they'd seen. One of the variables in the experiment was the following question (and variations of it): *About how fast were the cars going when they smashed into (or, collided/bumped/hit/contacted) each other?*

The researchers found that the verb used in the sentence would affect the response, with subjects recalling higher speeds when prompted by the words 'smashed' or 'collided', but much lower speeds when they read 'hit' or 'contacted'. Memories were bent by the expectations embedded in the question.

In the second experiment, 150 subjects watched a one-minute film that included a short scene of a multiple-car accident. Fifty subjects were then asked 'How fast were the cars going when they hit each other?' Another 50 were asked 'How fast were the cars going when they smashed into each other?', and the remaining 50 were not asked about car speeds at all.

One week later, all 150 subjects were invited back to answer a series of questions about the short film. They were not shown it again. The vital question was smuggled in among the others: 'Did you see any broken glass?' Those who had answered the question with 'smashed' in it a week before were more than twice as likely to recall seeing broken glass than the 'hit' or control group. But there was no broken glass. A single word had primed them and planted a memory.

A police officer told me about a sudden memory test he underwent years earlier in the academy. 'We were sitting at our desks in a classroom for some lesson, unrelated to what was about to happen. Then suddenly two guys storm in with guns. "This is a fucking hold-up!" they scream. "Get on the fucking floor!" Now, we all know it's a test, but it's still a bit of a shock. These two guys walk around the room, pointing their guns and screaming. We're beneath our desks. If someone looked up at them, they'd yell, "Stop fucking looking at me!" and point their gun. Then they were gone. What we had to do was sit and write everything we could remember about the two guys. What did they look like? What were they wearing? What weapons did they have? What did they say? What did they sound like? Who spoke first? Who was the leader? Whatever we could. So we do this, and I'm absolutely 100 per cent certain about everything I've written. So, they bring in the guys and they stand before the class. Well, fuck me. I'd got everything wrong. Age, colour of clothes. Everything. I couldn't believe it.'

———

By 1.30 on the morning of Friday 7 May, James Duggan had been interviewed for two hours. He had grown meeker, if that were possible. He was unable to account for himself, but his denials continued.

'Did you dump your jacket at the petrol station?'

'No.'

'But you've said that you went to the Mobil Quix on your way home.'

'Yeah.'

'Then how did your jacket end up there?'

'I don't know.'

'You don't know?'

'Nah, like, I went there but I didn't dump my jacket there.'

The implausibility of this was raked, fruitlessly, for a few minutes before the interview was terminated at 1.33 am.

'Can I get you a drink? Something to eat?' Bethell asked James.

'Can of Coke, please.'

'How are you feeling?'

'Unsettled at being accused of these things.'

James Duggan had held out for two hours, buffeted by conscience and authority. He had made inarticulate and unlikely revisions of history. He had offered both detail and obfuscation. It was a shabby and desperate performance, his boyishness offset by his insistent deception. He had played his role in a conversation that had felt, for the most part, like an interview, but had veered close to an interrogation at times. James was taken back to his cell.

Nearly two hours later, at 4.27 on Friday morning, a second interview began. There were two new investigators — Detective Sergeant Rob Wilde and Detective Senior Constable Adam Matson. Something had happened in the time between the end of the previous interview and the start of this one. We do not know what that was — whether there was any police coercion, a suggestion from a lawyer, or, simply, if isolated rumination had broken him. As it was, Duggan now sat at the table visibly distraught.

'You're happy to answer our questions?' Wilde asked.

'Yep, I want to,' James sniffled.

'In your own words, tell us what happened.'

'Gareth had nothing to do with this.' He was sobbing now, his chest heaving. 'I walked up to the park with Rebecca and we sat on the bollards and started kissing and the next thing I know I started choking her. I left her there and ran off and went to Mobil and dumped the jacket.'

'Why did you dump the jacket?'

'I don't know. I wasn't thinking.'

The question of the jacket might seem peripheral, but it speaks directly to James's intent and knowledge after the fact. That grey Quiksilver jacket had Rebecca's blood on it. Was that why James discarded it? And if so, was that because he knew she was dead? If he had seen the blood, he must have known that she was seriously injured. And given that, why didn't he call for help? Discarding the bloodied jacket placed James in a series of calculated attempts to cover up, derailing a narrative of an inexplicable brain-snap followed by shock and amnesia.

Wilde asked James to go back over the day. Back over *Jay and Silent Bob* and Xbox and VB and the pub. He was gentle — constantly reassuring him with the words 'It's okay, mate.' They made it back to the moment of murder. On the table before James was another can of Coke, and a box of tissues.

'Can you explain to me again what happened with Rebecca?'

'We sat down … on the bollards and we got with each other, started kissing. We both had a cigarette. I was smoking Peter Jacksons. I don't know what she was smoking. Then we kissed. And next thing I know I had her in a headlock. I don't know what I was doing. I ran to Mobil and threw the jacket away and bought some things and the dude behind the counter called a cab for me.'

'I know it's hard, James, but I need to ask you about what took place when you started kissing.'

James nodded, his head bowed. 'We were sitting. Then we stood up and I, I think, more kissing and then I started choking her and I couldn't stop. I don't know why.'

'Can you demonstrate what happened?'

'I got her in a headlock and started squeezing.'

'With what arm, mate?'

James indicated his right.

'Okay.'

'I didn't … I wouldn't … stop,' James was trembling, the words strained.

'What was she doing?'

'Nothing. Absolutely nothing. No sounds, nothing. Then she just slumped on the floor and I started running.' James seemed surprised by his recollection of this — the fact that she did nothing.

'How long were you kissing for?'

'Three, four minutes.'

'What did you want to happen when you were kissing?'

'Not sex. It never crossed my mind.'

'Why did you strangle her?'

'I don't know. My head was just spinning around and around. Everything was mixing together.'

'For how long?'

'I don't know. A few minutes.'

'Did you think that would kill her?'

'No. I wasn't thinking.'

'Did you kill her because she wouldn't have sex with you?'

'No.'

Wilde began to describe the scene. 'James, Rebecca was found naked from the waist down. Do you know anything about that?'

'No, I never touched her like that.'

It was 4.57 am, and James was breaking down. His head was on the desk. He was weeping.

'You okay, mate? You want a drink? We'll just stop the questions for a little while … You okay?'

'Nope,' the word was eerily stretched out. Haunted.

'Can you continue on?'

'I have to.'

'Why do you have to?'

'To get it out.'

'You understand that you're not obliged to answer any of my questions?'

'I understand.'

'So, you want to get it out?'

'Yep.'

'Why?'

'Because I want to know why I did it. I feel bad that—' [here, James's words become garbled].

'I know it's painful, but we need to figure out what happened. Rebecca was found naked from the waist down, her bra was twisted and her jumper was torn.'

'The [torn] top would've been when she fell and I was holding her. I didn't do the rest.'

Wilde patiently sketched the scene again, hoping to prompt Duggan's memory. Then he returned to Rebecca's torn cardigan.

'The [tearing of the] top would've been when she fell,' Duggan repeated, but he strenuously denied having unclothed her.

'Were you drunk, James?'

'No. I was feeling normal.'

'What about drugs?'

'I don't do drugs.' This was a lie.

At 5.13 am, having unsuccessfully tried to loosen

Duggan's amnesia, Wilde shifted from the night of the murder to the following day.

'When did you first become aware of the news?'

'That morning.'

'What were you feeling?'

'Nothing. I didn't even feel sad.'

'Were you excited?'

'Not at all.'

'Did you have sex with her at any stage?'

'No.'

'James, I have to be honest, the stripped underwear and clothing is a sticking point.'

James sniffled. 'I didn't do that,' he says.

Wilde asked Duggan if there was anything he would like to say before they concluded. 'Just that I'm sorry.' At 5.25 am, the interview was terminated.

Nearly two weeks later, on Wednesday 19 May, Detectives Wilde and Matson visited Duggan in Hakea Prison for another interview. This time, Duggan wore a plain black T-shirt. The detectives had secured Duggan's confession for the murder, but were no closer to determining his intent, or how it was that Rebecca's body had been interfered with. Duggan had always denied having anything to do with this. Wilde and Matson opened the interview with a description of the scene — the disrobement, the scattered items — as Duggan sat quietly, his head slightly lowered. When they finished, Duggan politely repeated his narrative of the bollard, cigarette, kiss, headlock, and departure. He told the officers again that he wasn't responsible for how the body was found. 'I've been speaking to a psychologist to help me understand, but I don't know why I did it.'

'Can you think about why her pants were removed?' Wilde asked.

'Nah.'

'Were you and Rebecca alone?'

'I think we were alone.'

'You *think*?'

This was strange. Duggan seemed both faltering and devious, clumsily introducing the prospect of a third party. It was unconvincing.

'Did you want to have sex with her, James?'

'No. I was just walking her home. I didn't want sex. Then I freaked out — I don't know why.'

'Did you find her attractive?'

James mumbled a denial.

'But you kissed her, so you must have found her attractive.'

'I just freaked out.'

'I think she rejected your advances.'

'I don't remember why I got her in a headlock.'

The detectives appeared annoyed; Duggan was sullen.

'James, let's go over where Rebecca's items were found. Her mobile phone was found in a drain on Limetree near your father's house. How did it get there when you said you took another route to the petrol station?'

'I don't know how the phone got there.'

'You're denying dumping Rebecca's phone?'

'Yes.'

'James, this is a little hard for us to believe.'

The denials worsened — became pathetic, petulant, implausible. James had already admitted going to the Mobil petrol station *and* dumping his bloodstained jacket there, but he was denying having dumped Rebecca's earrings *at the exact same spot as his jacket*.

'James, it's hard for us to comprehend how you dumped your jacket there, and not the phone and the earrings.'

'I have no idea how the earrings got there.'

The denials continued, becoming less and less articulate until they comprised merely shrugs of the shoulders.

This was odd, to say the least. Duggan admitted to the murder, admitted to running to Mobil, admitted to dumping his jacket there. But he denied dumping his jacket because he was discarding evidence (but couldn't say why he would otherwise have thrown away his clothes), and denied having dumped Rebecca's earrings, even though they were found in the same place as his jacket. Why? Was it shock? Was shock tampering with his memory? Or was there a strategy?

It seems peculiar that Duggan might recall some things from a specific time and not others — that he would remember dumping the jacket and not the earrings. What's more likely is that Duggan's denials were logical extensions of his principal denial: that he was sexually motivated and had stripped Rebecca from the waist down. There might be two reasons for this: first, that calculated attempts to hide evidence paints a worse picture of him — that, rather than a sudden, violent, and inexplicable collapse, here was a calculating killer. Second, if Duggan had removed the clothes (inviting inferences of sexual perversity), the disposal of her items at Mobil seems like the continuation of a pattern begun with the unclothing of the body and the wild scattering of her belongings around the scene.

On its own, it appears nonsensical to admit to a killing and to having gone to a petrol station afterwards, but to deny dropping the victim's earrings while he was there. But it becomes logical if Duggan sensed the detectives' belief that it was part of a pattern that included not only murder, but also sexual motivation *and* calculated concealment. It might defy logic to deny inconsequential details, but that's probably not how Duggan read it. They *weren't* irrelevant points — they were elements of a narrative that Duggan knew worsened the crime.

Rebecca's family refuse to believe that they kissed. They don't believe that her last moments were spent making a catastrophic misjudgement of character. It is nauseating to think that your daughter was intimate with her killer, however briefly. Rather, their belief is this: as they walked towards her home, Duggan thought he might get lucky. He 'got fresh', she rejected him, and was killed. At Hakea, the detectives thought similarly.

'I didn't know if she was dead when I left.'

'You didn't check for vital signs?'

'No.'

'Do you know how to check for vitals?'

'Yeah, you put your fingers on the neck ...'

'James, we find it highly unusual that somebody else would come along and take Rebecca's clothes off.'

'I have no idea about it.'

The detectives went back over the scene — the nakedness, the strewn items — and the fact that James was at Mobil but still denied discarding the earrings there. They were calm, but obviously tired of the farce. In response, Duggan said, 'I don't know' *ad nauseam*.

'Are you covering for somebody, James?'

'No.'

After forty minutes, the detectives ended the interview. They had gotten nowhere.

Duggan would remain in prison until his trial, nearly two years later. It would go to trial, despite his confession, because his lawyer could not agree to a plea with the state prosecutor. In Western Australia, unlike other jurisdictions, there are three levels at which Duggan could have been charged. In descending order of seriousness, they are wilful murder, murder, and manslaughter. The distinguishing feature between each is *intent* — in this case, did he strangle Rebecca with the intention of killing her, or merely harming her? Wilful murder would involve a level of premeditation.

Well before the trial, the defence made an offer to the state for Duggan to plead guilty to manslaughter. It was rejected. Then, three weeks before the trial began, they offered to plead to murder. It fell through. As Duggan's lawyer explained to the judge: 'The sticking point, I think, was exactly what facts we might plead to or might be agreed between us, but at the end of the day we never got that far down the track with the offer.' No doubt these disputed 'facts' included Duggan's involvement in undressing the body, which would present an additional and aggravating element to the crime.

In January 2005, the Ryles held a second funeral service back in Bolton, at St Matthew's church in the suburb of Little Lever. They brought with them some of their daughter's ashes. St Matthew's was where Rebecca was christened, and where her parents had been married 20 years earlier. Marie told local newspapers why they were having a second service: 'Rebecca wanted to come back to Bolton soon after we moved out there, so it is only right that we bring her back. She was also very close to her grandfather, so it will be nice for them to be buried together ... Many people, including my mother, who suffers from ill health, were unable to make the trip to Australia for the funeral. Rebecca had a lot of friends in Bolton, and it will be nice to see them again.'

Before they left on the long flight, Fran made a small box out of jarrah for Rebecca's ashes. He measured, sawed, and sanded with tears in his eyes. 'It was the hardest thing I've ever done,' he tells me.

Neither the church nor Rebecca's family had anticipated the enormous crowd of mourners. 'In England we were having the reception at the Conservative Club,'

Marie told me, 'and we asked how many they were going to cater for. They said, "about 50", and 400 people showed up,' she laughed. 'In the newspapers there were pictures of these huge lines of people waiting to light a candle. These numbers helped us.'

Those numbers were composed of different parts of the Bolton community — neighbours, old high-school friends and teachers, members of the Sea Cadets, and patients and staff of the hospice where Rebecca used to volunteer. They gathered silently as Fran spoke: 'Becky enriched all our lives ... She had a caring and thoughtful nature, and was determined to follow a career in nursing, a step that seemed the totally natural choice.'

As mourners filed up to the altar to light candles, Robbie Williams's 'She's the One' was played twice. At the end of the service, Fran walked down the aisle holding the wooden box, and Nick Cave's 'Into My Arms' came over the speakers. Beside the grave, where this part of Rebecca's ashes was buried, Fran's mother left a bouquet and a card that read: 'With a broken heart I whisper low. God Bless You Rebecca. I love you, Nanna.'

FIVE
SPEAK SOFTLY AND CARRY A BIG STICK

James Duggan's trial began on 7 February 2006 in the Supreme Court of Western Australia. It had been repeatedly delayed — the result of procedural logjams and court refurbishments — and each postponement was an intolerable pain to the Ryles. Before each nominal commencement date, the Ryles marshalled their strength, only to slump into torpor when the trial was re-scheduled. Clench, release, repeat. They were mentally shackled to the rough logistics of justice.

The Crown Prosecutor was Gillian Braddock, a British ex-pat who had received her law degree at Cambridge. Four years after this trial, she would be promoted to sit as a judge on the Western Australia District Court. Braddock's appointment as the Crown Prosecutor wasn't easy — Duggan's mother worked for the Director of Public Prosecutions (DPP), so a barrister had to be found elsewhere to represent the state. 'It was going to be done by the DPP,' Marie tells me, 'and then we got a letter or a phone call to say that it wasn't being handled by them anymore because there was a conflict of interest. It was being handed over to the Commonwealth.'

Tom Percy QC led the defence. Percy is something of a personality in Perth, a criminal-defence lawyer who has long appeared on popular radio shows and as the singer-songwriter for Celtic folk group Gang of Three. He is a divisive figure, strutting and cocksure, and naturally reviled by innumerable families of murder victims. This is an unavoidable fate for a criminal-defence lawyer, but Percy aggravates passions by being so flamboyantly unapologetic. It is obvious to say that due process requires defence lawyers to test weak evidence and shoddy police work, as it is to observe that victims' families will emotionally reject that duty. It is also obvious to say that the law's interpretation must be sober, a necessary contrast to the aggrieved souls embroiled in it.

But, for many years, Percy has committed the unpardonable sin of hubris. Enraptured by his own talent, Percy in court engages in a performance that appears to confer great pleasure to its actor. If we respect his role — and we must — it might seem churlish or ignorant to question the manner in which he acquits it. But what grated the Ryles was how total his performance was. They were desperate to see him acknowledge the moral complexity of his job; they wanted to see him conduct his duty gravely, not colourfully. But this sentiment seems anathema to Percy. The law is the law, and he has a job to do. There's no room for tender feelings. If he has to play the villain, so be it.

To the Ryles, he *is* a villain. 'I think he thought he was in a drama, an actor playing a role,' Marie told me. 'Arrogant. And he'd bring in his entourage. All these dolly birds. They must have been law students, don't get me wrong. But this one particular day, there were about four of them, and they all followed him in with their coffee and they sat down and court started. And they're sipping their coffee and talking and giggling. And I was mortified. I really was. We reported it, and I think the Victim Support Officer took it on. And it was taken to the judge, and then in the afternoon they weren't allowed back in. He was reprimanded for that. I mean, they were giggling, laughing. Total disrespect. I was so cross.'

'Percy's not my favourite guy,' Fran added. 'Fantastic intellect, I'll grant him that. But the thing that really stuck in my craw was that he said, on the scale of murders, it's not the most grievous. And I thought, *How can you say that?* For a bloke of his education, and alleged maturity, how can you think that? It's like ridicule.'

'At the end of the trial,' Marie said, upset, 'when he was found guilty, we overheard him say to someone [on the prosecution team] "So, you win." Yeah, thanks. He was trying to catch our eye, but I wouldn't even look at him.'

The trial was all about intent. Determining Duggan's purpose while he strangled Rebecca was the jury's principal task, the thing that would fix his conviction for wilful murder, murder, or manslaughter. The WA jurisdiction is unique in having the 'wilful murder' charge, defined as an act demonstrably intended to result in death. 'Murder' is a wilful act of violence that results in a fatality, but death cannot be proven to have been the aggressor's intention. These were the two charges on Duggan's indictment: if he were found innocent of them both, he would automatically be convicted of the lesser category of manslaughter.

Intent is distinct from motive, and the latter needn't be determined by a jury in order to find the accused guilty of wilful murder. The Crown Prosecutor, Gillian Braddock, was careful in her explanation of this to the jury: 'There really is only one issue to be determined in this case, and that's the intent of the accused, James Duggan, at the time that he, in his words, "choked" Rebecca Ryle, and the defence doesn't challenge those admissions.

'There's no doubt that asphyxiation by neck compression led to Rebecca Ryle's death, whether it be quickly or slowly. You don't have to be satisfied of any reason why James Duggan caused her death — of any motive. You don't have to find any theory or explanation apart from the elements of the offence ... There is no requirement that you find, as it were, a solution or answer to all the questions that as human beings we find raised by these circumstances.'

While forensic teams could find the exact causes of death — and the prosecution would submit those findings as evidence — what was occurring in Duggan's head as he caused that death was another matter. Percy stressed to the jury, as Braddock had, that the jury didn't have to discover a motive. But he differed with Braddock on how determinable Duggan's intent might have been. 'You see, what my learned friend says to you is abundantly correct,' Percy told the jury. 'Homicides don't have to have a motive. [For] some there are none.' But Percy added: 'How do you prove intent? You can't bring it along in a plastic bag like the plaster cast of the footprint or the little bag with earrings in and say, "Okay, well, we can prove that." You can't get the DNA expert to come along and say, "I have conducted some tests on him and I can tell you what his intent was." Intent is just a question of inference from the surrounding circumstances.'

Braddock disagreed. She argued that it was verifiable in this instance. 'Intent is as much a fact as anything else, only it's one that can't be photographed. In some instances it may be admitted to directly. You know what you intend when you say, "I'm going to the shops to get the vegetables", but not here in so many words. What is asked of you is to review the whole of the evidence, and bring that to bear on the question of intent.'

The prosecution's argument can be succinctly captured: Duggan was guilty of wilful murder, and the necessary intent could be divined from the forensic evidence, his calculating (if strange) response afterwards, and the sexual 'connotations' of the stripped body. In essence, this was the trinity of the argument, but Braddock detailed eight components of her case for the jury: the force of the strangulation, the condition of the body, Duggan's bizarre behaviour afterwards, the disposal of his jacket, the lies he told police in relation to the jacket, the broader lies he told police before his admission, his failure to admit to sexual motivation, and, finally, the opacity of Duggan's account.

These elements were of varying argumentative strength, but it was not specious to argue that the forensic evidence provided a glimpse of Duggan's mind at the point of strangulation. Investigative pathologist Dr Gerard Cadden testified about Rebecca's injuries, concluding, 'The intensity of the congested change is inconsistent with fleeting contact or transient contact with the neck surface because these changes are very obvious. It would lead one to suggest that it may have been some minutes that an unremitting compressive force was applied to the neck — some minutes.

'I will deal with the issue of time. The time of one to two minutes [suggested by Duggan as the approximate length of the strangulation], literally one to two minutes — 60 to 120 seconds — that time is very short. If it was one minute or two minutes and the pressure was relieved, you would have expected the person to possibly regain consciousness. Once one goes to three, four, or five minutes, the situation changes in that you are towards the time frame when some authors suggest that brain damage occurs.'

It was probably the most useful testimony for the prosecution. Braddock repeated it to the jury, adding: 'You might be able to conclude … that at the time he applied the pressure — that must have been applied to bring about the changes that Dr Cadden reported to you — that he intended to cause the death of Rebecca Ryle ... Putting any person in that position, not only are you likely to know what's likely to happen, but to sustain that, to maintain that, indicates a purpose in doing that.'

That purpose being murder.

Percy's defence rested upon two pillars. First, Duggan's intent was unknowable, perhaps even to himself, and certainly could not be proved beyond reasonable doubt. Second, there was a similar lack of evidence supporting Duggan's involvement with the unclothed body and frenzied crime scene, which might suggest to the jury a more sinister intent. He would implore the jury to find Duggan innocent of the two charges on the sheet.

Percy's argument would be informed by Duggan's police interviews; by his insistence that he had killed Rebecca, but did not intend to, and that he had nothing to do with the body after she slipped, unconscious, from his grip. This had been Duggan's story to investigators, and there was no evidence to suggest otherwise. Duggan's insistence would become his lawyer's.

The police interviews would become a text competitively interpreted by prosecution and defence. Both sides would cite it as either proof of intent, or its absence. Braddock proposed to the jury that Duggan's admissions to police, and his ensuing description, was a performance. A recitation. Braddock first discussed a third video, one in which Duggan is led around various scenes from that night. 'The third video is the one where you [get] taken through the scene. That really is very much a repetition, but on location, of things he has told the police in the second interview. It's quite graphic. It's a very unnatural situation for anybody to be in. He is very unemotional. It's very stilted. You might read from that, members of the jury, that he is not giving one iota more of information than he has already given. He is still holding out, you may conclude.

'When you come to the fourth layer of the interviewing process and 19 May in the setting of the custodial institution, you might think that the story has by then — it's absolutely set in concrete. You might have noticed when it was played right at the beginning he is asked, "What happened?" and he repeats twice almost exactly word for word in the same words. Certainly it might have struck you, members of the jury, as being, as I say, set, artificial. What he says is this:

> We had a cigarette, I think we kissed, and then we
> stood up and that's when I grabbed her in a headlock
> and choked her and then she, like, fell.

'Then, not very long after, he says exactly the same thing again when asked what actually took place:

> We had a cigarette, I think we were kissing, and then
> we stood up and that's when I, I think I grabbed her in
> the headlock then.

'It's a recitation, I would suggest. When he comes to this business, observe how he says it, "The next thing I know." It rings very hollow, members of the jury.'

Was Duggan 'holding out' behind a recitation? Behind a script composed of calculated admissions — the ones he knew he'd have to make, but which helped conceal the ones he refused to admit? The good propagandist knows to sprinkle some truth on the lies. But where Braddock was suspicious of Duggan's consistency, objective truth is, by definition, fixed. Based upon the logic of Braddock's suspicion alone, Duggan's unswerving retelling of that night isn't necessarily proof of his deceit.

Which is the gap Percy tried to leverage. Referring to the police interviews, Percy told the jury: 'You get a warts-and-all version of the story, don't you? This man, just taken out of his home the night after it happens, just tells it as it is. There's no rehearsed nature about that.

'It was his story from day one. It's still his position now, through me. That's his position. He doesn't know why he did it. It was not accompanied by any intent to kill her or cause her any serious injury ... What you heard from him, I suggest to you, is a pure version of his, untainted by lawyers or practice or rehearsal. What you see is what you get. You will have that in the jury room and you will be able to play it to yourselves again. Have a look at it, the second interview.'

Percy's largest gambit, though, was doubt. Doubt about the unclothing; more importantly, doubt about why Duggan strangled her. 'This is, I suggest to you, a baffling case. In the last six days, I suggest to you, we just haven't got anywhere near the answer; you nor me. My friend [Braddock] is right, as I have said, when she says there is no requirement, and her Honour will tell you this, to prove motive in a murder, and indeed there is no motive suggested here.

'You can be pretty comfortable in your verdict sometimes as a jury if there is a motive and you can say, "Well, that's why and that's how and that's the intention that he had," but here you have just got nothing. From start to finish, you have just got nothing. You have got an unlawful killing. You have got a manslaughter, I want to suggest to you. From start to finish it hasn't risen above that. When you look at your board in there [the jury room] and you look at the word "proof", ask yourself what proof is there of murder, let alone what proof there is of wilful murder.'

Percy also suggested the involvement of a third party, and while he didn't do so explicitly, the obvious inference was that Gareth Phillips could have participated in the posthumous disturbance of the body. Days earlier, an anxious and bitter Phillips took the stand and was grilled repeatedly by Percy over inconsistencies in his statements to police. The vast amounts of alcohol involved that night — and the fact that Phillips was stoned during his police interviews — didn't help.

'You told [police] you thought you had got home probably about 10.00 pm?' Percy asked Phillips.

'Yes.'

'Would you accept that that's probably true?'

'No.'

'No?'

'Because I don't really know,' Phillips replied.

'Why did you tell police you got home about 10.00 pm?'

'Have you been through 10 hours of interrogation?' Phillips asked angrily.

'I'm not here to answer questions. You tell me,' Percy responded.

'Because they made me feel like I had done something wrong.'

Moments later, Percy zeroed in on another inconsistency.

'Thinking about it now, when do you think you probably got home that night?'

'Between ten and twelve o'clock.'

'Did you speak to Michaela — that's James's mother?'

'Yes, I did.'

'What did you talk about?'

'She asked me, "Where's James?" when I got home, and I said, "I think he's at the pub."'

'You didn't tell her that at all, did you?' Percy shot back.

'Yes, I did.'

'You said to Michaela, "I don't know where he is", didn't you?'

Confused, Phillips repeated Percy's line back to him. '"I don't know where he is"?'

Percy clarified. 'Michaela said: "Where's James?" You said: "I don't know where he is."'

'I could have said that,' admitted Phillips.

'A minute ago you said to the jury that you told Michaela, when asked, that he was at the pub. What did you say? You said you didn't know where he was, or did you say he was at the pub? What was your answer to Michaela's question?'

'I don't know, mate.'

It may have been a small, common blip of memory, and absolutely inconsequential if it had occurred in an everyday conversation. But under the gaze of a Queen's Counsel, this slight contradiction hinted at grave implications. Percy resumed his examination.

'I want you to think about this. You have undertaken to tell the truth in this court, haven't you?'

'Yes. That's why — I don't know. I can't tell you the truth.'

'I know it's a long time ago, isn't it?' Percy briefly shifted to good, sympathetic cop.

'Yes.'

'Do you remember what you told the police in your written statement?'

'No.'

'You have had it with you today and you have read it today, haven't you?'

'It doesn't say in there.'

'I suggest to you that it says this in paragraph 36. If you want to see it, you let me know. Paragraph 36: "My bedroom has a padlock on it …"'

'Yes, I can remember that,' Phillips interrupted.

Percy continued reading from Phillips's statement. "'... and I was making some noise when I got home, and I recall seeing James's mum, who asked if I knew where James was." That's what you told police, didn't you?'

'Yes,' admitted Phillips.

'Paragraph 37: "I told her that I didn't know." Is that what you told police in your written statement?'

'Yes.'

'Is that true or false?'

'It's true.'

'A minute ago I think you told the jury, didn't you, that you told James's mum that he was at the pub. Why did you say that?'

'I don't know.'

Percy never spelled out Phillips's supposed complicity that night. He just left these contradictions hanging — a suggestion that they were not regular imperfections of memory, but signs of a rotten conscience. Phillips later groused to Percy that 'you're good at twisting things, eh?' Unflappable, Percy responded, 'If I'm doing anything wrong, people in this court will tell me.'

Marie Ryle told me that Phillips's testimony was bubbling with anger and frustration. He clearly did not want to be there. He resented being embroiled. He snarled at Duggan as he left the stand. Marie remembers him saying something like, 'You know you fucking did it.'

In Percy's closing arguments, he returned to Phillips on the matter of the crime scene — the unclothed body and scattered belongings. He was sowing doubt in the jury — could they emphatically state that a third party *hadn't* come along after Duggan had fled the scene?

'The witness Phillips — and again what you draw of his complicity or otherwise in this case is a matter for you, but there are some odd aspects of his evidence, I think it has to be said. My suggestion to you is that any overview of his evidence does give us the impression that he was trying to distance himself from any interaction with the deceased girl. You remember that? He was at some pains to say that he had nothing to do with her.

'When the police put it to him in his interview the day after, he said he was positive that he had had nothing to do with her. That has to be wrong, doesn't it, because a number of the witnesses at The Boat had put him talking to the girl. He was at some pains to do this in front of you. I asked him whether he was trying to tell the police the truth and he said yes. I put it to him that the police asked him the question, "You're sure, are you, that you have never met this girl?" Answer, "I am positive." I asked him why he did that. "Well," he says, "I was intoxicated when I had that interview with the police." I put it to him he was trying to distance himself from the girl. Again he didn't say he didn't know whether he had met the girl or he couldn't be sure; he was positive:

Q: Why didn't you tell them that in the video?
A: Because I don't have much memory of it.
Q: You didn't have much memory of it?
A: And I was intoxicated when I had that interview.

'I went on to say it was 24 hours since he had had a drink. He says, well, he had been smoking marijuana. You may well think nothing turns on that. I suggest to you the undeniable inference is that he was trying to distance himself from the events in question. What time did he get home? He told the police he got home at 10.00 pm. We know beyond any doubt, any doubt at all, he didn't get home until very, very much later. What he was doing, none of us will ever know, but it certainly wasn't 10.00 pm.

'It got worse than that, didn't it? Mrs Duggan asked him when he came in, "Where's James?" He says, "I don't know." Why would you say that? He knew precisely where James was. He was at The Boat tavern or on his way home. "Where's James?" she says. "I don't know." Make of that what you will. I suggest to you that when he told — in his police statement he said, and in his evidence in this court, that James told him later that afternoon the girl's clothes were found on the roof. Well, he hadn't told the police that in his interview, and he admits that. He was at a loss to explain any of these discrepancies.'

What Percy went on to say in his closing statements has stayed with Gareth Phillips. Today he is still angry about his suggested implication. Again, Percy was washing the case with doubt. He circled back to the threshold of 'proof', stressing to the jury that there was still so much they didn't know.

'[Braddock] makes the comment that it's virtually inconceivable that anyone other than the person who killed the deceased girl left her in that condition or dealt with her possessions. I suggest to you: is that right? Is that necessarily right, knowing what we know about a few people's whereabouts that night? It's a question for you.

'What I suggest to you is that the evidence relating to Gareth Phillips may well pose more questions than it answers. The case, I suggest to you, is not at all, with respect, as open and shut as my learned friend puts to you.'

I tried contacting Phillips for a year. I tried the obvious stop first — Facebook — leaving messages on his multiple accounts. Nothing. I tracked down friends of his, and left messages there. I tried possible places of employment, but they were all dead ends. I got hold of email addresses for old school mates, and tried them. Finally, a message got through to him via a friend. Obviously, the message was distorted, because I received this alarmed response:

> Hey Martin, my name is Gareth and I have been informed by a friend that you have been asking questions about me. This disturbs me a little. Who are you and why are you asking these questions?

I was appalled that I had upset him, and responded immediately. I introduced myself again, and pointed out that I had tried him directly before giving up and trying his friends and acquaintances. I directed him to the number of private Facebook messages that he had not seen. Then ... nothing.

I emailed him again six weeks later, inquiring once more if he might share his memories of that night and of living with Duggan. His response was curt:

No thanks, I'm not interested — I'm a busy family man with five kids. James has already fucked up my life and I don't want to go into it again. I was treated like I was a criminal, and it had nothing to do with me. Just turned out I was the unlucky one who lived at a murderer's house; so no, I'm not interested, thanks.

Not long after the murder, Phillips bumped into Marie Ryle at the local shops. 'You have to believe me, I had nothing to do with this,' he said. Marie accepted his words.

On 16 February 2006, the jury found James Robert Duggan not guilty on Count 1 of wilful murder, but guilty on the second count of murder. He would face sentencing three months later, when the motivation for his crime would be plumbed. Fran and Marie Ryle had hoped for a conviction of wilful murder, and their disappointment was compounded by a gross administrative error: their victim impact statements had been lost by the court, never finding their way into the hands of the judge.

'We had so much pressure put on us to do these statements,' Marie told me. 'They said to us: "It'll go to the judge, and she'll take that into account." It took days to do. The boys did theirs, too. We handed them in. It's a very hard thing to do, a victim impact statement. So we took them in on the first day, handed them in, and were told they would be passed on to the judge. Anyway, when they came to do the summary at the end, the judge says, "Well, I've not heard anything from the victim's family." We'd written these things, and they'd never even got to the judge. It was a slap in the face.'

Fran added: 'I found it hard to do. I kept it as objective as I could. I tried hard to articulate it. You sob your heart out doing it. It was very tough for the boys to do. It was like pulling teeth. And we never found where they ended up. There was no resolution.'

As the verdict was delivered, some detectives wept.

On 24 April 2006, James Duggan returned to court to face sentencing. It was an opportunity for the prosecution to submit arguments of aggravating circumstances — elements of the crime and the criminal that demanded the judge hand down a sentence towards the harsher end of what was available.* It was also, naturally, an opportunity for the defence to submit mitigating arguments: age, remorse, capacity for rehabilitation.

The prosecution's argument had changed. During the trial itself, the state tried to persuade the jury that Duggan had been sexually motivated — that Rebecca had been

---

* What's available is fairly limited to Western Australian judges who, in matters of murder, are legislatively mandated to enforce a life sentence. The judge, however, can set the minimum term between the statutory limits of seven and 14 years.

murdered after rejecting his advances. It aligned with the family's belief, and the belief of the investigating officers. But come sentencing time, the state seemed to accept that there was insufficient evidence to push for it as an aggravating feature. It was left a mystery.

'Your Honour ... the State's position is that the facts that should be found are that the circumstances in which the deceased was discovered and the disposition of her property are all matters in which the accused was the active agent; that is to say, how the scene was discovered was in effect how he left it,' the prosecutor said.

'Your Honour, it would therefore seem, without going into any speculation, we have a situation that is, as my learned friend has stated, as much an enigma at the end of these proceedings as it was at the outset. We are no better placed than we were to understand the mechanism by which these events came about; that is to say, the psychological mechanism or precipitating cause.'

It was a marked change from the trial, when the state argued in its closing statements: 'This is the sexual connotation part of it. This is strange, you might think, members of the jury. James Duggan admits to strangling her but not to taking her knickers off or to any sexual activity that might have involved some undressing. *I would suggest he has got some real problems here.* We know that he has not got a girlfriend, that he is not good with girls, no girlfriend as far as his mum knows.' [My emphasis.]

During sentencing, Duggan's lawyer, Tom Percy, reiterated the absence of any evidence of sexual assault.

'His position has always been that he at no time undressed the deceased, nor did he have anything to do with the dissemination of her personal items or the way in which she was actually found, with one of the sleeves of the cardigan between her legs.

'Significantly in that regard, there's no DNA or fingerprint evidence which might connect him to that. Similarly, we say it's of very significant importance there is no evidence of sexual assault.'

Justice Jenkins ruled more philosophically than legally on the reason for the murder. 'As to your motive and reason for killing Ms Ryle, you admit to having none. None of the experts who examined you or spoke to you are able to give a substantiated opinion as to your motive and reason for killing Ms Ryle. The State urged the jury at least to find that you killed her because she had rebuffed your sexual advances. I'm not prepared to find that you had such a motive.

'As I will discuss shortly, even though I find that you did interfere with Ms Ryle's body and clothing to some extent, I do not accept that this means that your intention was to sexually assault Ms Ryle or that you were angry with her for rejecting you. The emotion that motivated your crimes seems to be much stronger than that that would be consequent upon a virtual stranger rejecting your advances.

'It seems to me that to assume that there was sexual intention on your behalf simplifies human actions and emotions in a manner that is unwarranted. I simply do not know why you did what you did, and to assign a motive to you is simply to speculate.'

Sex is a shortcut. It features prominently in our logical fallacies, our confusion about correlation. So it is tempting, if grandiose, to interpret the judge's remarks as an existential defence of us all or, at least, a rebuke to our tendency to simplify in our desire to explain. We are capable of many things, and for myriad reasons — not all of which are explicable, even to ourselves.

The spectre of sex watched over the trial of James Duggan, as it had in police interviews with him. So, too, in Mindarie, where locals erroneously spoke of the rape of Rebecca, presuming that sexual perversity preceded the killing. In the neighbourhood, the state of undress of the body was evidence of rape; the murder, proof that Duggan wanted to silence the victim. Speak to people from the area today, and many still talk of 'the rape and murder of that young girl'.

Despite the lack of forensic evidence indicating sexual interference, the state of undress provided police, the prosecution, and the Ryle family with a compelling indication of motive. As we'll see, this was difficult in an evidentiary sense for the trial. But it's also a deeply inadequate way of explaining murder. The sex-murder has become a trope — two elements of sordidness twinned in our public imagination so thoroughly that we no longer ask if criminal lustfulness is a direct cause of murder. We just accept — or assume — that it is. They've become inseparable. One thing, seemingly naturally, leads to another. Why did he do it? Sex. End of story. The vast continuum of human motivation and depravity is ignored in favour of designating it as 'sexually motivated'. It was precisely this simplification that Justice Jenkins rejected in her sentencing remarks.

Regardless, the judge was satisfied, beyond a reasonable doubt, that Duggan *was* responsible for removing Rebecca's clothing. 'Given your bizarre murder of Ms Ryle, the fact that you knew at the time of your second video record of [police] interview that the top had been ripped, your removal of and the dumping of the earrings and the telephone, among other things, in my view lead me to the conclusion beyond reasonable doubt that it was you who did remove her clothing and interfered with the clothing on the top half of her body and were responsible for strewing her belongings about the area.'

In her sentencing remarks, Justice Jenkins raised another issue that aggravated the crime. It was something that had perplexed me, my brother, and just about anyone else I spoke to about the case — Duggan's apparent calmness at the petrol station. Justice Jenkins told Duggan, 'After you had choked Ms Ryle you did not know whether she was alive or dead, according again to what you told the police in your second record of video. Despite that, you then left the scene and went to a petrol station ... You called a taxi from the station and had to wait there approximately one hour before it arrived. You spent a considerable amount of time inside the service station shop talking to the assistant. Surveillance cameras recorded your behaviour whilst you were there.

'It aggravates your offences that you failed to obtain any assistance for Ms Ryle whilst you were at or after you left the scene. You had a mobile phone and money, which you could have used to make a phone call. It was also chilling to see your behaviour whilst in the shop, chatting to the assistant and buying things for yourself, knowing all the while that you had left Ms Ryle to die at the school.'

When police first asked the petrol-station assistant about Duggan, he would've named any number of different customers from that night as the likely suspect. But the scrawny kid who wanted a taxi? No way. The police must have had it wrong.

You can spend a lot of time thinking about the hour that Duggan spent at Mobil Quix. The amiable, ingratiating conversation with Luke Richards. The multiple purchases — food, drink, porn, and trinkets — and the fact that those purchases were staggered over an hour. The stubbornness with which he held onto Gareth's shoes; the fact that, even after the murder, returning the shoes still seemed an important thing for him to do. There is also, of course, the disposal of his jacket and Rebecca's earrings; but despite the clumsiness of his disposal of that evidence, it seems more explicable, or expected.

The rest of his behaviour is not. Psychologists, witnesses, lawyers, and those who knew Duggan have scoured that hour for significance, for clues to motive, mindset, compassion, and calculation. My brother had considered it, too. 'I can imagine he was trying to be cool, calm, and collected — not like he'd just done a murder,' Cameron told me. 'That's all I could imagine when I heard those stories that he'd chatted calmly to a petrol-station attendant. Like nothing had happened. And also that the guy he spoke to didn't think it was weird. I can imagine him in this drunken stupor thinking he can outsmart the cops in some way.

'If he had done it [the murder] in this blackout phase, where he lost control of himself, why is he calculatedly taking things off her and acting in this stage afterwards? That fits into my original idea of who he was and why I didn't want my friends hanging out with him.'

Cameron continued: 'Can you imagine — it's hard — but can you imagine how you'd feel if you had done something like that? If you had blacked out and you woke up and all of a sudden you had just killed this girl? It would be impossible to act in any other way but to feel completely sick. You'd go into shock, wouldn't you? You wouldn't be able to act normal. You just wouldn't be able to have a conversation. It's nuts. I don't get it. Unless he just decided — he made a decision at the time that he was going to get away with it. And that was his plan. To act normal. But obviously there's some sort of emotional problem there if you can do that. If you can disconnect yourself from that. It just shows complete disregard for any emotion. It's scary.'

Nothing in James's life suggested an ability to exercise an outsized will in order to quell despair and affect normality. To me, that hour invites amateurish appraisals of psychopathy. There was nothing to suppress, because there was nothing there. It was all scorched earth, an inner landscape untouched by empathy.

But when you commit a murder, you are subject to a battery of psychological assessment. Not long after his arrest and confession, while he was remanded at Hakea Prison, a psychologist met with Duggan. Another clinician met with him prior to the trial — yet another before the sentencing hearings. They yielded almost nothing. During sentencing, all sides expressed frustration at the psych report's opacity on the question of Duggan's motive.

It's worth quoting extensively from the sentencing hearing on this matter.

Mr Percy: Just for the record, I confirm the contents and the accuracy of the detail in those [psychological] reports and I don't have any submission in relation to the contents of them. Essentially they don't take the matter a lot further than what was before us previously.

Justice Jenkins: No, perhaps regrettably.

Mr Percy: It is. In preliminary discussions with my learned friend [the Crown prosecutor, Ms. Braddock] before your Honour came in, despite the best of intentions on the part of all those people and their best endeavours, the matter remains an enigma.

Only a few minutes later, Percy returned to the enigma. 'Initially when confronted with this case, myself and my instructors looked for some evidence of some psychiatric or psychological imbalance which might answer some of the questions, but to date we have been unsuccessful, as have the relevant practitioners. He has, it must be said, no relevant psychiatric illness. He was examined before his trial, as far back as August 2004, but Dr Patchett has had a very good look at him and he concludes in his report that Mr Duggan doesn't suffer from any significant psychiatric functioning; no difficulty has been found at a neuropsychological level.

'He has also been assessed by Dr Connor, and your Honour will have seen the observations that are made there. Indeed, none of the medical assessment of him really brings us any closer to understanding why he finds himself in the position he's in.'

The psychological reports are suppressed — other than these expressions of frustration at their paucity — but it seems likely that Duggan would have been an uncooperative patient. A gifted therapist isn't enough — it requires a subject willing to give himself to the process, to painfully choose disclosure over avoidance. On the matter of why he killed Rebecca, Duggan would have to try to untangle himself. But Duggan was far from suited to this process. Reticent and emotionally stunted, revelation was likely also deterred by shock and self-loathing. To the court, the prospect of his rehabilitation was conditional on his demonstrating insight about the crime — but would Duggan have either the skill or the courage to explore his shadows? Or would the clinician be met with profound obstinacy?

Consistent with other police interviews with killers I've seen — and consistent with the stories that homicide detectives have told me — murderers are rarely voluble about the actual moment of killing. They can speak clearly about the moments before and after. They can cooperatively provide a timeline. They can express regret and mortification. But rarely can they describe the moment itself with any clarity. Quite often, the shock of recognition — or reckoning — is too great, and probably sometimes the forces of shock and localised amnesia are deployed to soften the horror. Unless they are psychopaths, it is in the interest of killers to give themselves over to a narrative of hot, inchoate madness — something temporary and spontaneous. For Duggan, things were simply 'spinning around and around'.

'My immediate feeling is that there cannot be a "murder without motive",' Ron Spielman told me. Spielman is a retired psychiatrist. 'To my mind, all human behaviour is motivated by some personal "meaning" — no matter how outlandish, bizarre or cruel — it means "something" to the given individual being considered ... If the psych assessments of him didn't reveal anything, then they weren't adequate assessments.'

Spielman had been in touch with me after reading some of my newspaper reports on the psychology of young radicalised killers. Melbourne had provided the Islamic State with two teenage recruits — Adam Dahman and Jake Bilardi — who would violently offer their lives in the hope of taking others'. Dahman had walked into a crowded Baghdad market with a bomb strapped to him. He killed five. Bilardi reportedly drove an explosives-laden jeep into an Iraqi checkpoint, killing himself but no others. They were both 18.

Spielman and I chatted about the cases before he invited me to attend the 2015 Freud Conference, held at Melbourne University. This year's theme was religious extremism. Spielman had also been a psychoanalyst, before his recent retirement. I paused before I indulged my curiosity: how could a man of science, a psychiatrist, also be a practitioner of a methodology famously resistant to verification? Among many therapists, psychoanalysis is now viewed as a kind of pretentious voodoo. I knew that Freud had largely vanished from most psychology courses — on university campuses his legacy was sustained by literary and cultural studies. 'Psychoanalytic concepts are — or should be — integral to psychiatry,' Spielman told me, 'in that understanding the *person* with the mental problems should be paramount. Unfortunately, modern psychiatry — and "modern" patients — are impatient and want symptom relief rather than understanding, which theoretically should lead to symptom relief. Problem is it takes too long and is too costly. Medications are "easier" — but don't deal with the underlying issues.'

While I had Spielman on the phone, I couldn't

help but ask his opinion about Duggan. Which was fraught. Spielman had never heard of the case, much less examined the perpetrator. But I was curious. For fear of leading the witness, I withheld certain particulars of Duggan's life, but provided Spielman with a sketch of the crime. 'Well first,' Spielman said after listening to me, 'for there to be such an extreme act as a murder, there must — to my mind — be dysfunctional upbringing for sufficient rage and lack of empathy to permit a killing. Rage toward one or both parental figures coupled with a developmental "deficiency" in respect of acquiring a capacity to empathise with an "other".

'Second, for a young man to murder a woman, there must be an inadequately developed sense of healthy masculine identity and an inability to respectfully relate to a woman. Which leads to point three: if his own sexual identity is insecure, he is especially vulnerable to feeling rejected by a woman he may approach sexually. This could unleash an outburst of murderous rage as a result of feeling humiliated and inadequate.'

I was impressed. He'd identified the same trinity of clues to Duggan's psyche that I had. But then I became cynical. Was this the charlatanism of Freud — to offer clichés as perspicacity? If you spoke often enough in generalities, something would stick eventually.

Except that Spielman wasn't speaking generally: he was quite specific. My cynicism gave way to an opposite thought: perhaps Freudian clichés were not homilies, but useful archetypes; perhaps Freud had isolated universal patterns of our neurosis. We may find the predictability of psychoanalysis's fixations amusing, but the Freudian would retort that they are predictable because we are.

In many conversations with Spielman — I went on to attend the conference with him — I thought I came to better understand why Freud was now the province of literary study. After our first conversation on the phone, I'd provided Spielman with a draft of this book. From that, he'd offered to expand upon his theories of Duggan's mind. And what I thought was: psychoanalysis is a sort of literary criticism, a divination and mapping of our 'deep structures', based upon a close and ideologically prescribed reading of ourselves. Psychoanalysis was an act of transforming symbols into narrative, and vice versa. 'Psychoanalysis does inform much literary criticism,' Spielman said. 'Both are concerned with understanding human states of mind and motivations for behaviour. "Analysis" of literary works concerns itself with both the mind of the author and the minds of the "characters" in the work.'

One of the conceits of a criminal trial is that the two respective portraits of the accused — offered by the defence and prosecution — are complete, but that both can't be accurate at the same time. We saw this clearly in the trial of Oscar Pistorius where, depending upon the interpretation of the evidence, there would be a different interpretation of the man. The alleged character and the alleged crime were in lockstep. One led to the other.

The two arguments about what happened the night that Pistorius shot and killed his lover, Reeva Steenkamp, were: (a) Pistorius woke in his bedroom in near darkness, and left his bed without the aid of his prosthetic legs to shut the room's balcony door. Hearing what he thought was someone entering the bathroom window, and believing it to be an intruder, Pistorius seized his gun from under the bed that he believed still occupied the sleeping Steenkamp. Fearing for his life, Pistorius blasted four times through the toilet door. (b) Following a dispute with his lover, Pistorius knowingly shot Steenkamp through the toilet door.

Flowing from these arguments are the respective profiles of the man who committed either (a) or (b). The man responsible for the 'tragic accident' is a man made hyper-sensitive to his vulnerability as a result of a double-amputation when he was one, the death of his mother when he was fifteen, and his being a wealthy celebrity in a country that records 15,000 murders every year. He is a man whose celebrated narrative is defined by overcoming a permanent sense of vulnerability. The tragedy here is that by fearing the worst, he made the worst happen.

The other man, the one responsible for murder, is violently petulant, immature, and feels deeply entitled. He has a history of reckless gun use and a propensity to angrily defer responsibility. According to phone texts tendered in the trial, Steenkamp complained to Pistorius about his jealousy and dark moods.

The conceit here is two-fold: each profile is a complete

rendering of the soul of Oscar Pistorius, and each profile is mutually exclusive. But if you combine the two profiles, you're probably nearer to the 'truth'.

James Duggan's lawyer had his own profile of his client, compromised though it was by the mystery of motive. He was a normal suburban boy, with no prior criminal convictions, who had committed an insensible, inexplicable act. 'He was 19 at the time of the offence,' Percy told the judge, 'and this person, we would say that your Honour is entitled to accept, is of previous good character. His referees describe him as a normal teenager, trustworthy, loyal, and helpful.'

Here we have a series of truths — the lack of a criminal record, the optimistic and supportive references tendered by his parents — but not *the* truth. The admissibility threshold of courts prevents hearsay as evidence. Necessarily, in a court there appear only officially sanctioned facts. The court cannot be the accused's exhaustive biographer, needling out all of the complexity and nuance of a man. No, Duggan did not have a criminal record — but there's no official document about people who probably should have one. There's no admissible record of idle nights spent smoking weed in car parks, no record of James's involvement in house parties crashed by machete-wielding dealers. Nor is there any legal argument to support the idea that any of these things are relevant.

Percy's simple profile of his client as a knockabout kid was reinforced by the absence of convictions. In Percy's hands, the lack of a criminal record came to have serious symbolic value. It suggested a kid previously unsullied by criminality. The absence of prior convictions reinforced the defence's narrative that the murder was a brutal aberration, and so the chances for rehabilitation were promising. All this was the prelude to asking the judge to consider a lighter sentence.

But in responding to Percy's suggestion of normality, the judge said, 'A "normal teenager" and yet the extent of alcohol and cannabis abuse could not be described as normal, could it? I mean, we see people like that all the time in these courts but one would hope that out there in the community it's not regarded as normal for teenagers to have that extent of alcohol and cannabis abuse.'

'I think what the referees simply say,' Percy said, 'is he was a knockabout boy and essentially there was nothing radically unusual about him.'

This exaggerated faith in the accuracy of referees' reports — written largely by his family, and others invested in his release — is part of the performance of a criminal trial. The stories from the street aren't admissible in an adversarial trial, and rightly so, but we are asked to accept as pure the reports from his family.

What is interesting about the judge's rejection of Duggan's putative normality is that she cites the *very thing that was utterly normal* in the place he lived — cannabis and alcohol use. Surely the one thing that argues for his abnormality is his killing of a young woman for no discernible reason.

When I read to my brother these suggestions of normality, his response seemed to get much closer to Duggan's character than the judge could. 'There's all these accounts of him being a normal kid, but normal kids don't murder people,' Cameron told me. 'Take the drugs and alcohol out of it — that was normal for the area. But what kid takes a girl and does something like that? It's not normal. All accounts of him being a normal teenager should be thrown out. Obviously, there were other things going on. That picture of the normal teenager wasn't true.

'I don't remember his cannabis use being on the everyday side. I wouldn't have said … I don't have any memory of him smoking. I'm sure he did, but I don't think it was that often. Some of the people we hung out with were smoking every day. He didn't drink every day, either. But when he did drink, he'd binge drink. We all did.'

Let's pause on the respective ideas of 'normality' here. The judge seems to have mistaken the word for 'regrettable', because teenagers using booze and drugs in the suburbs is among the most normal things I know. Her response seems more aspirational than accurate.

Percy's calculated notion of normality is curious, too. It suggests that one can be 'normal' and still commit something heinous. That one can commit something that flourishes from nowhere — a Big Bang of criminality, an explosion triggered in a vacuum. The notion is calculated, because Percy is attempting to stress the weird aberration of the murder, rather than it being an expression of something that had long germinated inside Duggan. The prosecution's argument was simpler: 'If we do not know why he did this, we do not know he won't do it again,' argued Braddock.

My brother's appreciation of whether he was normal or not was different. The murder itself demanded we reappraise Duggan. Everything in him was now suspect, a potential ingredient for murder. The very fact of the killing revoked any ideas we might have had about his normality. What he did was aberrant, and he must have carried the seeds of that aberration within him all along — invisible, perhaps, even to himself.

'My words cannot adequately describe the awful nature of your crime,' Justice Jenkins told Duggan at the end of the sentencing hearings. 'For no apparent reason you took a young woman's life by literally choking it out of her and then you abandoned her without making any attempt to obtain help for her or give her assistance. She died not of old age in the presence of her family, but at an indecently young age, alone and degraded.

'Your offence is every parent's worst nightmare. Every loving parent dreads that their child will naively go with someone who can apparently be trusted, only to be the subject of awful violence. Ms Ryle's parents must live with that nightmare for the rest of their lives. Nothing I can do today will change that. I'm sure it will always seem to them a great injustice that you will still be a relatively young person when you become eligible for release, whereas they will never be released from their suffering.'

The judge was required to set Duggan's term at between seven and fourteen years. As she noted, there was
no discretion to alter these limits. Justice Jenkins asked
Duggan to stand. 'James Robert Duggan, in relation
to the offence of the murder of Rebecca Louise Ryle, I
sentence you to life imprisonment. I set the minimum
term of eleven-and-a-half years' imprisonment.'

A court officer approached Fran and Marie, whispering that the press were assembled outside — did they
want to speak to them? The prospect intimidated Marie.
She had no idea how to translate the swirl of relief,
disappointment, and infinite sadness into a statement.
But Fran wanted to try, and it made Marie nervous. She
knew her husband was fixated on Duggan, knew he was
full of disgust and fury. But Fran was determined to speak
to the cameras, so Marie stood by him. She squeezed
his hand very hard, an invisible way of requesting his
restraint. The fury survived, but Fran spoke quietly. 'He
shows only sadness that he was caught and he's facing
a jail sentence. He does not care, he's lacking all human
characteristics, as far as I can see,' Fran said.

'However long this animal serves behind bars will
never be long enough for us. He's destroyed a wonderful
young lady and he's destroyed our lives, and we just
cannot understand why he attacked her with such
ferocity, without provocation, without mercy. He robbed
her, he interfered with the body. He totally degraded our
daughter, and we had to listen to seven days of that, and
we are very angry and very sad.'

Fran later told me of that speech that he felt as if he'd 'kept my powder dry. That's the thing: try not to be hysterical. Strong words, softly spoken. Was it Truman who said, "Speak softly, and carry a big stick"?'

The Ryles feared that their case was corrosive to Detective Wheatley. For years, she stayed in touch with them, once attending a large family gathering at the Ryle house. Drink in hand, Fran thanked her again for an attentiveness he was convinced exceeded her professional obligations. 'There must be an emotional cost to you,' he said.

Wheatley deflected the suggestion. She didn't want the family's pain pinched by a sense of debt. 'Yeah, but it just goes with the job,' she replied modestly.

Fran was determined to impress upon her their gratitude and admiration. 'How many murders have you worked on?' he asked.

'Several.'

'And which one was the hardest?'

'This one,' Wheatley admitted, and she talked about a hierarchy of feeling, how some murder victims were violent themselves, complicit in their deaths through drugs or gangs. 'Low-lifes,' she may have called them to Fran. The murder of Rebecca was different.

The Ryles would write a letter to the commissioner of WA Police, recommending Wheatley for a promotion. But Wheatley had grown weary of her job. She left it, and now runs a café. When she's not there, she's likely

spending time with her horses. She hasn't seen the Ryles
for a while.

'She was great,' Fran recalled. 'A very strong woman.
She guided us through it. Was with us 24/7. She was
there every day of the trial. An exceptional person.'

The Ryles were in servitude to their pain. But they
also understood the burden of police officers, realising
what the rest of us rarely acknowledge: the psychic costs
of the job.

I met with Adam Oswald, the first police officer at the
scene of Rebecca Ryle's murder. I wanted to discuss the
case with him, but also to ask for his thoughts on police
trauma. Oswald has left the force, and now works as a
lawyer for a private firm. I met him in his Joondalup
office. The offices were far from the glittering citadels of
corporate law — they were small, drab, unpretentious,
and nestled in a village of shops that included a greasy-
spoon café, a printer-cartridge store, and a real-estate
agency. They were within walking distance of the local
police station and magistrates' court. At Cleveland
and Co., Oswald practises a variety of law that wasn't
permissible with WA Police — criminal, civil, and
migration. On any given day, Oswald can handle traffic
infringements, domestic violence, or property disputes.

On his desk sits a plaque with his name and qualifi-
cations engraved on it. The walls are empty, the office
small, and Oswald plainspoken. After we discussed the
case, I asked him whether he had ever met the Ryle

family, given that they lived so close to each other.

'No. As a police witness, you don't contact other witnesses. Otherwise you can get contamination. I've seen it in court every day — you have to quarantine yourself so you don't bring in any other memories that may cloud yours. That's my memory, that's what's occurred, that's how I bring it out. It's clear. So even today I can recall where things were. You see something, you remember it. You put it to one side at the end of the day. You have to. You can't dwell on it. You can't bring it into your family. You have to be able to quarantine. It's something I learnt when I was in the army. You see enough horrific things to say, "Well, that's one part of my life", and put it out of sight.'

'Do you do that successfully, you think?'

'I think so. I've seen some pretty horrendous things. So … touch wood, I haven't had to do anything yet. Being able to compartmentalise things and put it to one side is a big plus. Some people can't do it, and they burn out real quick.'

'And they leave the force,' I say.

'Yep.'

I asked Oswald if this strict quarantining of experience had numbed him to surprise or shock. 'No. You still get surprised. You still get shocked. But that's a different side of it. Once you get over the surprise and shock, you have to switch into work mode, and then you can compartmentalise. Everyone gets shocked. I think when I went past my house to pick up the tarpaulin [to obscure

Rebecca's body at the scene] the wife just looked at me white-faced. It shows on everybody. But it's how you deal with it afterwards, alright? I think the army training helps a lot with that. Doing service, you're exposed to that sort of thing. You learn to deal with it. You still get shocked and surprised by some of the things you see. But you can't dwell on it. It'll burn you out. I think some of the police departments now have a two-year maximum. That's it. Changeover. Stop the burnout. With regular psych reviews.'

SIX
THE PEBBLE MEN

The first time I knocked on the Ryles' door, I turned and faced the school. I knew the proximity of the murder site, but it took my standing on the threshold of the house to understand just how close it was. I was astonished, and desperate to inquire about their reasons for staying. I had distantly and ignorantly surmised the decision as unhealthy.

Fran opened the door, releasing two large Labradors. 'Alright, mate?' He smiled, and extended his hand. 'Don't worry about them,' he said as the dogs pounced on me. He ruffled their coats. Fran was warm and enfolding, despite his apparent anxiety. I followed him past the den, on the wall of which was a large photo of Rebecca. Fran headed to the kitchen, and offered to take my bag. 'Can I get you a drink, mate? Tea, water, lager?' I wanted a beer — we both did — but asked for water. He directed me outside to the patio while he put my bag away and got the drinks. I took a seat and removed my phone, a pen, and my notebook.

I realised that I'd seen no one else in the house, but as I thought this Fran came outside and said, 'Marie's just in her room. She'll be out soon,' and he placed a pint glass half-filled with water in front of me. The white logo of The Boat was impressed upon it. There were reminders everywhere. Across the road was ground zero, and for some time the obscenity must have denuded their lives. But here they were still, the bougainvillea blooming upon the dividing wall, and the sunshine mingling with the swimming pool. It was still home.

Fran opened the bar fridge near the outside table I was sitting at, and retrieved a stubby of Beck's. 'You sure you don't want one, mate?' I said that I did, and smiled wanly at the hollowness of my earlier gesture. And so it continued for two beers — a polite refusal to explicitly confront the reasons for my being there, and their reasons for having me. In the English manner, aided by lager, we would creep politely towards rapport or disharmony. Certainly I wanted to explain myself, and speak to their anxieties, but I wanted to wait until Marie joined us. So Fran and I talked about football, the weather. I patted the Labradors. We waited.

Marie came outside. Where Fran exuded geniality, Marie couldn't disguise her trepidation. I cringed. I was responsible for this. Perhaps Marie's agreement was in fact Fran's? Perhaps there had never been a unified decision to meet me, but a unilateral one, and I was now experiencing a marital rupture I had helped create. But I was wrong. Fran and Marie were equally anxious

— as they were both equally interested in meeting me. Their feelings just manifested differently. 'It's actually an honour you've chosen Becky as a subject,' Marie said as she sipped from a glass of white wine. I was relieved.

The Ryles distinguished themselves quickly, and in doing so dictated how they would appear in this book. Fran spoke most, but not because he was overbearing. He often deferred to his wife or, realising the limitations of his perspective, asked Marie what her interpretation was. They debated points — sometimes sharply, often playfully.

Fran was expansive and cerebral, his speech a mix of British argot, famous quotes, and anecdotes. He could riff in passages of genuine eloquence. I came to believe his expansiveness was partially the result of having served in the navy. As a young man, his profession had obliged him to participate in global politics. He spent time stationed in the Middle East and the Americas, met members of foreign services, and fought in a war. Whether it was in combat or factories, Fran developed loyalties within harsh environments. But he was never a slave or automaton in these masculine cultures. He pondered their organising principles and his involvement in them.

Marie's world was family. She was fiercely loyal and loving, and most happy when serving her clan. She conceived of herself as the stable matriarch — the fulcrum of the family. She found pleasure and identity in domestic rituals. Marie had less to say than Fran, but not because she felt less. She felt enormously. The two were very different, but recognised and joked about those differences. They sparred jocularly, each ceding to the other's respective gifts. I admired them as a couple.

I explained to them that they were under no obligation to answer my questions. The injunction felt harsh, an abrupt scratching of the groove Fran and I had carved out before Marie's arrival. But I needed to establish parameters — or, more accurately, to assure the Ryles that they could set them. I reiterated my reasons for writing the book. Their nervous expectation was that I would immediately begin a blunt, cold inquiry into the murder. But I wanted to know about *them* — where they came from, why they had left England. As we spoke about their lives, I sensed them relaxing. The alcohol helped, too.

I pointed at the empty pint glass and apologised for what I was about to ask: why were they still here? They didn't flinch or take exception to my question. They never did. And the reminders were often more brutal than mere pint glasses. A few times, Fran had been out the front of their house only to hear locals casually remark to others about the significance of the place. 'This is where that girl got murdered,' they'd say, pointing at the plaque, and Fran would contemplate shouting out and introducing to them the name of 'that girl'.

After a few hours, Fran went inside to grab the boys, Chris and Andrew. They obliged. They were both young men and, despite the age difference between them, I couldn't pick the eldest. They were polite, but their body language betrayed their discomfort. Andrew had long black hair and wore a black Metallica T-shirt. On his forearm was a tattoo of a heart with a dagger through it. Beneath it was a fluttering ribbon, upon which was written: 'You're my Wonderwall'. It was a tribute to Rebecca. Fearing his father's shock or intervention, he had waited until Fran was overseas before he got inked. He had it done on Rebecca's birthday. 'Disclosure,' said Fran, 'I did actually think that when Rebecca died, a year or so after, that I might have something done on my chest. But then I sobered up. I was in the arms of Bacchus at the time … But I spent 22 years in the navy, and everyone had tattoos, and everyone regretted it. Eventually.'

Chris had short hair and a handsome face. Fran had shown me his artwork earlier, and he had a coil-like intensity, suggesting a battery of raw and thoughtful opinions. Both of them were bright and creative, and could speak about suffering with an unusual depth and self-awareness. It is easy to be sycophantic here — easy to offer flattering descriptions as a *quid pro quo* for them welcoming me into their home. But they spoke with genuine insight and soulfulness, even if they didn't trust me or the circumstance. I liked them as much as I liked their parents.

The reason they had the pint glass from The Boat was because Chris used to work there. Again, I was astonished. Chris had experienced his own variation on the pains of proximity when he was having a lads' night at the pub next door to The Boat, the Indian Ocean Brewery. One guy started talking about having lived in the area for years, and then started on the 'chick who was raped and murdered'.

'She wasn't raped,' Chris corrected.

'How do you know?'

'Because she was my sister.'

The bar manager intervened and advised the tactless young man to never mention Rebecca's death there again. 'The blood boiled a bit,' Chris told me. 'But he's not a bad lad. Dopey, but you can kind of let it go.'

Such was the place. Rebecca had worked at the shopping centre where Duggan briefly pushed trolleys with my brother. Duggan's stepfather lived around the corner from the Ryles until his death a few years later. Adam Oswald lived just as close. Andy was at primary school with Duggan's stepbrother. Chris would go to the same college as his other stepbrother, Matt. And Matt would later apply to work at The Boat — while Chris was still working there. 'When they took on Matt,' Chris says, 'it was pretty uncomfortable. We had a chat to the manager … It was strange, because he was sort of a mutual friend. I think he's gone back to England now. But my friends used to know him from school. For a while we were moving in similar circles, but never actually meeting. I kept my distance. But he's as much a victim as we were, in a way.'

One day, some time after her daughter's death, Marie was doing some grocery shopping at the local store. As she pushed her trolley perpendicular to the aisles, she thought she caught a flash of someone — down the other end — duck out of sight. Puzzled, she slowed down and waited for the person to reappear on the other side. It was James Duggan's mother.

The Ryles had only been here a short time when Rebecca was killed, but instantaneously it became a sacred place for them. 'At first it was weird,' Chris said. 'I didn't want to be here, I wanted to be back in England — we'd only been here for six months, so that was understandable. But in a way, I think, we have a more important connection round here; it's more ours than it is most people's.'

To leave, they thought, would be to abandon Rebecca. Their family had been dismembered, but here they were spiritually whole. To be sure, life organised around a patch of turf, sorrowfully transfigured, seems dangerous. But there were reasons of enlightened pragmatism, too — they refused to be intimidated by ghosts when the reasons for their move still held. I thought this was a rare and healthy response. 'We're absolutely comfortable here,' Fran told me. 'I like it. The beach, and my snorkelling, my pottery workshop, my pool, my shed — and I do shed things, you know? I just feel comfortable, really. I suppose we could afford a bigger house, or something else, but it just feels right for me. There might come a time when we feel like we can move on and move away, but we're quite settled.'

Margaret Thatcher had decided to defend her islands. So Fran Ryle was off to war, sailing into one of the 20th century's least-likely conflicts. The Royal Navy's HMS *Glamorgan* would bear him to what Ronald Reagan had described as an 'ice-cold bunch of rocks': the Falkland Islands, 400 miles from the South American coast, 850 miles from the Antarctic Circle, and some 8,000 miles from home.

The Falklands may well be an ice-cold bunch of rocks, but they remain fiercely contested between the British — who have held sovereignty over the islands since 1833 — and the Argentinians, who argued that the 1833 possession was illegal. In 1982, the Argentinians were increasingly bellicose, but privately Thatcher still believed that an invasion was unlikely: 'I never, never expected the Argentinians to invade ... it would have been absurd and ridiculous.' But instructed by the military dictator Leopoldo Galtieri, a murderous and unpopular figure at home, Argentinian troops seized the island on 2 April. There had been no declaration of war, and details were scarce — the governor of the island had simply sent London a short and enigmatic telegraph: 'We have new friends.'

By the time the invasion had been confirmed, Thatcher was already preparing a taskforce to reclaim the islands. The House of Commons was called for an emergency session on Saturday 3 April, and the prime minister took the floor:

We are here because, for the first time for many years, British sovereign territory has been invaded by a foreign power. After several days of rising tension in our relations with Argentina, that country's armed forces attacked the Falkland Islands yesterday and established military control of the islands … It is the Government's objective to see that the islands are freed from occupation and are returned to British administration at the earliest possible moment.

Fran Ryle was just 22, and a young naval mechanic on the *Glamorgan*. They were berthed in Gibraltar when the orders came. He was unmarried, but had a girlfriend back home in Bolton. Like Fran, the *Glamorgan* came from England's industrial north, hammered and welded into existence in a construction yard in Newcastle. It was a County-class, making it smaller and faster than other warships, designed to provide air defence for larger ships in the fleet.

When they arrived, it was hell. The *Glamorgan*'s usual role was to provide supporting fire for the ground troops — strafing Argentinian positions from the sea. In turn, the HMS *Glamorgan* became the target of Argentinian Mirage jets that screamed overhead, unleashing massive payloads. So far, the bombs had all narrowly missed.

Among this, another young man on the *Glamorgan* — the captain's secretary, David Tinker — found the grace to write this observation home:

Certainly the trivia of life and the important things are all brought to mind by this. And how much trivia are at the forefront of normal life and the important things put away, or not done, or left to do later and then forgotten. Here, certainly, the material things are unimportant and human things, values, and ways of life are thought about by everybody.

Seventy-two days of war had passed, and so far the *Glamorgan* was untouched. Others in the fleet weren't so lucky. The HMS *Sheffield*, another County-class destroyer, had been struck by an Exocet missile, fired from a fighter jet. It blew a hole in the hull, killing 20 men, and sinking the ship six days later. While the surviving crew waited to be rescued, their ship listing wildly, the captain led them in a rendition of Monty Python's 'Always Look On the Bright Side of Life'.

The war was coming to a close. The *Glamorgan*'s final task was to provide night-time naval fire while an army unit — 45 Commando — attempted to take the mountain range, Two Sisters. Fran's ship was 18 miles from shore.

At around 2.30 am on 12 June, the Argentinians fired a land-based Exocet missile towards the *Glamorgan*. The ship's navigator glimpsed a brilliant dash of light tracing over the shore. He rang the alarm, chaff was discharged, and the ship was forced to make a dramatic turn. But the defensive moves came too late, and the missile ploughed through the ship and exploded in the galley. Shrapnel ricocheted into the hangar, smashing into a Wessex helicopter and causing it to explode. In all, 13 men died. One of them was David Tinker.

There were flames, smoke, and seawater everywhere. There were severely burnt survivors. One officer was pinned beneath smouldering wreckage. It was dark. Confusion reigned. Fran, like most of the others, was putting out fires and pumping water — there was a chance that they might go the way of the *Sheffield*.

In a few hours, they had avoided sinking. But it was now time to bury the dead. Fran said goodbye to his friends as they sunk to the ocean deep, 160 miles east of the Falkland Islands. The next day, the Argentinians surrendered.

Fran took another sip of beer and looked at me. *This* is what he would rather experience — every day for the rest of his life — than the murder of his daughter. 'I came back from war damaged,' he told me. 'It was hellish. But it was nothing compared to the ferocity of the grief of losing Becky.'

The ferocity of grief. It is a sharp description, and memorable. I have thought about it often. The ferocity of grief was not adequately captured in the initial newspaper reports: 'A 19-year-old woman found murdered 150m from her Mindarie home yesterday may have been the victim of a sex attack. The part-time student's semi-naked body was found about 6.45am in the grounds of Mindarie Primary School by a local resident walking his dog … A short time later, the mother was being comforted by neighbours and spoken to by police.' [Various newspaper articles at the time reported different distances, but the crime scene was closer to 50 than 150m from the house.]

Our newspaper articles on murder can't get close; they're too thin and indelicate. Each one sounds like another, diligently but crudely hemming to a formula: 'young woman murdered; family mourns'. It is not always the reporters' fault. The stories are blunted by the dictates of space, style, and currency, but we rarely learn anything but the crudest outlines — these are sketches on napkins.

For all of the words written about the death of Rebecca Ryle, it was a photographer that best captured the ferocity of the Ryles' grief — a portrait of Fran and Marie sitting on this patio, their glazed eyes speaking of their captivity.

The Ryles are conservative — they have faith that traditional institutions confer civic stability and coherence. They are not slavish in their beliefs, are both wary of the misuse of power and the indelicacy of justice. But they are both monarchists, for instance, and Fran speaks often about the essential elegance of the Magna Carta and the Westminster system. But when Rebecca died, Fran became soaked in a murderous reverie. It disturbed his conception of himself as a gentle man, and disrupted his belief in a tradition of impartial justice.

There was one prominent fantasy, as specific as it was brutal. It played repeatedly in his head, as if animated by something independent of him. Fran kidnaps Duggan — assisted by chloroform and ropes — and dumps him in the boot of a car that also contains the tools for his torture. Saws, pliers, hammers. Maybe a blowtorch. Then Fran drives out to the bush. En route, Duggan regains consciousness but not his freedom, bound and panicking in his dark cell. He knows where he is, but not where he's going. He wonders, will I be killed or just injured? And would he guess the identity and motivation of his captor as the car speeds over the gravel roads?

They arrive at their remote destination. Fran turns the engine off. He can hear Duggan's muffled cries and his desperate kicking of the boot's canopy. Fran relishes the control, muses contentedly on how he has recreated the founding terror, refracted it back upon the monster. He opens the boot and stares at his daughter's killer. They're both a long way from England. A landscape of March flies and eucalypts. Fran can't hear the birdsong. Neither of them can.

Fran introduces himself. If Duggan had any doubt about the reasons for his captivity — or the likely outcome — it's banished now. He struggles again, and Fran grabs him roughly and dumps him to the ground. Then he collects his toolbox, filled with instruments once put to constructive use but now reserved for torture. There commences sustained barbarism — cutting, sawing, burning. Fran then wraps piano wire around Duggan's neck and ties him to a tree. 'Wild animals and flies would do the rest,' Fran told me.

This fantasy was relayed quietly and shamefully, by a man who only earlier had picked up the artwork of his son from the dining table and rhapsodised tenderly on its quality. 'I struggled because of the anger,' Fran told me. 'I spent a lot of time wanting to kill him. That was quite a dark phase, the first few months.

'I spent a lot of time speaking to a psychiatrist about the fantasies. I saw him for about two-and-a-half years. It was useful. He told me that it's okay that I want to kill him or see him dead — it's totally understandable — but the problem comes when you start sharpening knives, buying rifles, or stalking his mother. Or wanting to stalk him when he gets out of jail. But the anger itself is perfectly natural. I saw the guy every couple of months, but initially it was once a month.

'I've seen a lot of violence in one way or another, but I've never hurt anything or anyone for the sake of it. I don't like hurting things. I'd rather create something than destroy something. But I could've cheerfully killed him without any remorse at that time.'

How well can you reconcile yourself to meaninglessness? For the Ryles, this isn't a mere thought-experiment — their health hinges upon it. They are left with the hideous collision of the real (a murder) with an abstraction (meaninglessness). It is now their life's work to resign themselves to the meaninglessness of the act itself (not its consequences) while living a life in which they can create and respond to their own meaning. Keats called it 'negative capability' — the ability to accept ambivalence or irresolution. 'To dwell in uncertainty without an irritable reaching for certainty.'

Fran continued to work at the naval shipyard in the months after Rebecca's death. His colleagues were a 'mixed bunch'. There were ex-navy guys like himself. Some had been lifelong tradesmen, moving from one contract to another. There was a South African engineer; another bloke with a Sicilian background. The Sicilian drove a lovingly restored Monaro, and while Fran detected a sharp edge to him, they developed a jocular rapport. Each would pronounce certain ethnic stereotypes of themselves in a sort of collegial performance. 'He used to do the Mafia thing,' Fran said, 'and I'd do the stupid Pom thing. We got along, bizarrely. We had this banter.'

But after the murder, Fran sensed his colleague's toughness might be something more sinister. He was dark and retributive, and had contacts in the shadows. One day, he approached Fran on the docks. 'Franco, just say the word and we'll get him sorted.'

'What do you mean "sorted"?' Fran asked, though he felt he knew.

'Off the government rations, do you know what I mean?'

Fran did. It was an offer to have his shameful fantasies realised. What were the odds? Fran's private schism — between civilised man and our animal other — was being publicly tested. Would his commitment to impartial justice defeat his urge to balance a blood debt? It was one thing to speak about this hypothetically in the safety of his therapist's room, but another to face it here. *Bloody hell*, Fran thought, before saying diplomatically to his colleague, 'Well, let's just leave it to Her Majesty's wisdom.'

Well into our beer, Fran told me, 'It wouldn't have surprised me if he could have done it. And I thought, *I don't want to be a part of that, actually.* It sounds square, or old-fashioned, but I believe in the law and due process. I don't believe in vendettas. We're just ordinary Joes, plodding along ... I thought, *Let the judicial system do what it does, bang him up, and don't waste your life on a shit like that. It's just not worth it. It'll destroy your life like a cancer.*'

Six months after the murder, Fran's contract at the shipyard ended. He found work as a repairman at the Swan brewery on the bank of the Swan River. He met Terry there, a New Zealander whose toddler son had been killed by his babysitter. Terry recommended to Fran a homicide-support group that met in East Perth. He told Marie, and they decided to try it. They weren't coping. They thought of themselves as drunk zombies. So they went one night after work, and found a room of about 30 people arranged in a circle. As debutant members, the Ryles were asked to stand and introduce themselves. When they sat back down and the others spoke, they realised the terrible sum of resignation and anguish. It was bracing. Unhealthy. Among them were families of suspected victims of a serial killer — their loved ones never found, nor a culprit convicted. The Ryles knew they'd made a mistake. 'They were dwelling on it,' Fran said. 'It had become this all-consuming thing. They were garnering their memories, and their hatreds and bitterness. And I said to Marie as we were driving home, "We can't do this. We can't let this define us. We can't live in that environment of hatred and venom. We have to be more positive and proactive. Do affirming things, rather than polishing our hatred." We were lucky in that they got Duggan straightaway, and we got a trial and we got him banged up. We got Becky back, and she wasn't mutilated or anything like that. Relatively, it was a good situation compared to not having found the body, not having the time to grieve. The whole issue is different. I did feel sorry for these guys — don't get me wrong — but they were in a downward spiral. I couldn't see any glimmer of hope for them to get out of this pit of despair.'

Much of that despair sprung from an inability to accept what had happened. Many in the group, much as the Ryles had, were bitterly examining the what-ifs and hypotheticals — the endless tiny variations that might have prevented the murder. The Ryles, like their counterparts in the support group, could have indulged infinitude: what if she hadn't gone out, but watched telly with them that evening? What if she had taken the lift offered to her by Nathan? What if Gary had accepted Duggan's request to join them at Bar 120? What if Gareth hadn't run off after the fight? What if Rebecca wasn't so open, so trusting? An entire book could index the smallest quirks of fate that would result in Rebecca being alive. And such is the power of grief — and the swiftness of our mental computations — that countless what-ifs can be imagined in moments.

The what-if is a meat hook on which victims' families almost always catch themselves. They can spend a lifetime trying to wriggle off it. For the rest of us, the alternate realities of a murder can be glibly discussed around the water cooler; for the families, it can become a toxic obsession.

Such obsessive rumination can also transform itself into activism — a passionate quest to correct the perceived flaws of the justice system, which either helped the killing happen, or retarded full and proper justice.

About two years after the death of Rebecca, Fran was sitting in a fold-up chair on his front lawn, his dog beside him. He had just been made redundant from a factory, and was contemplating his next move. Just then, a local approached with his dog, and suddenly the two pets began excitedly investigating each other. The stranger wandered over and exchanged pleasantries with Fran. Then there was a pause. 'Listen,' the man said, 'I always wanted to make contact with you and tell you how sorry I was. I put flowers here, but I never wanted to knock on your door. It wouldn't be appropriate, imposing like that. I have a daughter called Rebecca, too.'

Fran was touched. Mark, the stranger, introduced himself. 'How are you for work?' he asked. Fran admitted that he had just lost his job and wasn't sure what to do next. 'Would you be interested in disability care?' Mark asked. Fran was. He wanted a change, and this sounded like a practical and satisfying tribute to Rebecca. He could make a difference. But he wasn't qualified. How could he pivot to such a different career?

'I could help you get a job,' Mark said. And he did.

It seemed a good fit. Fran is attentive, modest, and empathic. And he knows pain intimately. But the job would introduce him to yet more suffering and spiritual destitution. Marie wondered if it would be too much for him. Later, there were times when Fran wondered, too. One elderly client of his was ravaged by years of drink and depression. Fran told me this client had been brutalised as a child. Among other cruelties, he had been flogged by his stepmother with a horsewhip. One day, after renewing his drinking, the gentleman hung himself from a tree in his front yard. His son discovered him in time, and cut him down.

Fran spent a lot of time with him in hospital. He brought the man clean clothes and magazines. He talked with him for hours. After the man's daughter-in-law told Fran that Centrelink was demanding the client look for work, Fran assumed an advocacy role and negotiated with the welfare agency. 'I spoke to Centrelink and told them they were making a guy seek work who is not fit for work,' Fran remembered. 'I told them he's exhausted. Let him go out to pasture. And so they did, eventually.'

It was harrowing for Fran — both witnessing the suffering and its bureaucratic refractions — but he saw the results of his work. Later, the man's daughter-in-law called to thank him. 'He's retired now, and spending time with his grandchildren and making wooden toys for them,' she said. She also told Fran that he had been the only man who had stood up for him his whole life. 'Well, I can do stuff like that, rather than fantasising about murdering Duggan in barbaric ways,' Fran told me.

Marie was influential in this transition, encouraging Fran to take the chance, and supporting him once he had. She saw herself as a football manager, improving the aspirations and achievements of her brethren. That Fran still works as a carer today is largely attributable to Marie. As it was for his next big move.

Davis Station, the busiest of Australia's research stations in Antarctica, lies 2,250 nautical miles from Perth. Fran had dreamt about it for years — the wild remoteness, its brutal otherness. He suspected Antarctica could both enchant and challenge him. He had spoken about it for some time, and Marie's eventual advice was blunt: 'Just bloody do it, you wimp. You only have one life.'

There was a time he couldn't have gone, when the family was in crisis. But after seven years, they were clambering off the lifeboat they'd all shared. Fran and Marie felt the timing was right, and so he began applying for positions on the station as an engineer. If successful, he would be posted for six months. It was a long time, but Marie had experienced similar absences when Fran was in the navy. In 2011, Fran was notified that he'd been successful.

Over summer, Davis Station can host up to 150 staff. During Fran's period, it was half that. There were plumbers, photographers, and physicists; electricians, engineers, and meteorologists. There were carpenters and a chef. Staff are designated 'expeditioners', and, despite their respective professions, are all required to perform rostered duties — cleaning, sweeping, brewing beer. Fran was impressed. No matter your age or education, everyone had to empty the kitchen slops. 'Very quirky,' Fran said. 'Very Australian. Very egalitarian. We would go to other stations. We went to the Chinese station and Indian station, and they're so hierarchical. But in our camp everyone takes a turn washing pots, or making beer. There's no rank.'

On Wednesdays, an expeditioner would provide a mini lecture to the group about their area of expertise. One Wednesday, a satellite expert gave an enthusiastic but technically dense lecture. Afterwards, Fran turned towards the tradies. 'Did you understand that?' he asked. They shook their heads.

Fran worked hard on the tools, but on weekends he would book a helicopter and be dropped off in remoter areas. There was a spooky barrenness to the snowfields, and the weather — even in summer — could drop to 20 below. But the silence and solitude was useful to him. It was unlike anything he'd experienced. It was both bracing and beautiful, but he wished the phone-link home worked better. Marie couldn't wait for him to get back. When he was gone in the navy, she had young children with her. But now the boys were older, and they all passed her 'like ships in the night'. Marie was happiest with a full nest.

Fran had formally eulogised his daughter at least three times: at two funerals and her school's service. But eulogies assume multiple forms, and they never end. The Ryles eulogised Rebecca when they caught themselves laughing and stopped. They eulogised her when they stopped eating together at the dinner table because of the empty chair. They eulogised her each time they met pleasure and dismissed it as morally gauche.

These tributes and self-abasements were strongest around sex. Sex was stained. Impure. And for two reasons: not only were its resultant pleasures questionable, but the sexual implications of their daughter's murder had contaminated it. It was a squalid place, the act of sex hopelessly invoking Rebecca's killer. The Ryles were aware of the consequences this could have for their marriage.

It was Marie who first broached this with me. By this point, over two meetings in a week, we had been talking for about 15 hours. What the writer Helen Garner once described as the 'charge of serious psychic energy that can flash between a subject and an interviewer — what the Jungians call "The spark that ignites and connects"' had happened. Marie's initial trepidation the first time we met had by now been replaced with a candour that even Fran was hesitant about providing. While we sat outside, the sons were inside cooking dinner. I include the whole of our exchange here, unexpurgated. Their voices and honesty require no aid, and deserve no dilution.

'If your sex life is damaged,' Fran said, sipping his beer, 'then it's a core part of marriage or any relationship. Let's be honest, it's just part of a relationship. I'm not being flippant. It's who we are. I had this lovely, warm, satisfying relationship, and it's just soiled, damaged now.'

'He got frustrated because I wouldn't even entertain it,' Marie replied.

'The whole point for me was why it was damaged — it wasn't that we were having fun.'

They paused, deep in thought, and I spoke haltingly. 'Depression and grief can destroy libido, but you're saying that on top of that it was the quality of your daughter's death — the sexual motivation of it — that sullied it for you?' I asked.

'Yes,' Marie hissed the word softly, for emphasis.

'It was contamination,' Fran said. 'I still find it hard to this day. In the early days, I thought, *I shouldn't be doing this, my daughter's dead*. It didn't seem right. It felt wrong. It was a long, long time afterwards that we had sex.'

'That was my fault,' Marie said, gently.

'No, no, no, no, it wasn't. I didn't want it in that context.'

Unhelpfully, I added, 'This seems like a massive thing, but it's never discussed.'

'It's a big facet of grief,' Fran agreed.

'I don't suppose many people speak about these things,' Marie said. 'We've got to be frank, don't we? Francis, we've gotta be frank.' She laughed at the play on her husband's name.

'I could have played away when I was in the navy, but I didn't. I like the exclusivity of a relationship. I don't want a one-night stand. So it took a long time with Marie, but I was willing to wait patiently.'

'I wouldn't have been happy about it, but I wouldn't have blamed him if he'd have gone somewhere else,' Marie told me. 'I wouldn't have been happy, I would've probably divorced him. But I would have blamed myself for it.'

'But I wouldn't have done that,' Fran told Marie. 'Sex without you isn't valid to me.'

Marie turned to me. 'He's very loyal. Very loyal.'

'It wasn't in my bag, the one-night stand,' Fran joked. 'I tried it once in '78 and didn't like it … I like the warmth and security of an exclusive relationship.'

Marie took a sip of her white wine. 'We have our ups and downs, but … we've had some shit and hard times, and we'll slag each other off sometimes, but at the end of the day we are soulmates. I couldn't imagine life without him. And I think he thinks the same about me.'

Fran agreed.

'He'll get obsessive, he needs to know everything, but sometimes there's nothing to know.'

'That's true. That's fair enough. I need to try to understand everything in my tiny mind.'

'Do you still struggle with pleasure?' I asked them.

'Yes,' Marie said.

'How can I describe it?' Fran wondered. 'It's just taken the sparkle off so many aspects of our life, really. There was a good mate of mine — I sailed with this guy for a couple of years. Alec. A real intellectual, this guy. He was an ardent left-winger. And I was a bit more right wing. So we had this political banter going on. Bit of cut and thrust in our discussion. He was well-read, and — how can I put it? — he used to love going to rock concerts, always reading stuff, and ...' Fran trailed away.

'You've lost your point, haven't you?' Marie asked him, smiling.

'Yeah,' Fran chuckled.

'I've reached a certain age when the menopause has started and it ... I need a bit of *50 Shades of Grey*. Have you read it?' Marie asked me.

I had not.

'The actual storyline is quite good,' she said.

Chris called out from inside, 'No, it's not!'

Marie called back. 'Have you read it?'

'Only portions.'

'What do you mean by portions?' I yelled.

'Just the dirty bits,' Marie answered for him. 'The storyline's good. His mother was a crack whore, and he was adopted by doctors, and ... the doctors got him into the sado-masochistic sex, and he just thought that's how women wanted to be treated. He meets this girl and she went so far, but he realised she wasn't into it, but he loved her and he changed his ways a little bit, but then she mellows and agrees to some of his ways.'

'Is it fair to say that sex is mostly in the mind?' Fran asked.

'Yes, I would agree to that,' Marie said.

'It's mostly about imagination,' Fran said. 'The more explicit stuff you see or read and the less sensuous it is, I suppose. There's a time and place for everything. When you're young and foolish.'

'We had some raunchy moments,' Marie suggested.

'Oh, we did. Without a doubt, and very nice, too,' Fran said.

'I remember a stormy night in Windy Harbour,' Marie said.

'Where's Windy Harbour?' I asked.

'Lancashire,' Fran told me.

'It was a caravan site,' Marie said. 'We shouldn't be telling you all this,' she laughs.

'The point is,' said Fran, 'we always had a good physical relationship.'

'You're remarkably open,' I said.

'Well, we're not normally,' Marie replied. 'But we thought we have to be upfront. I had no intention of talking about sex — he's gonna bollock me later.'

'Not at all,' Fran promised.

'It's a very important point,' Marie said.

'If you accept that 80 per cent of couples who lose a child to homicide their relationships break down, well … you can totally understand. Because it just devastates every aspect of your life. You can't function at work, you're drinking a lot — you might lose your job to that,' Fran told me.

'And we did all that,' Marie said.

'Yes. We could've quite easily been sacked.'

'Oh, yeah,' Marie agreed. 'I remember one particular morning, and I drove to work and I felt so rough, and I set everything up and then went and lay on the treatment bed. I just needed to sleep. And I think I was just lying down for five minutes. I was still drunk. Thank god it only happened the once. But I was out of it.'

'They were the early days, weren't they?' Fran said to Marie.

'Yeah.'

'Then we got to thinking that we had to knock it on the head. Get serious,' Fran told me.

'I still feel ashamed about it. I'll never forget that,' Marie said.

'It was the early, dark days. An overwhelming blackness,' Fran said, his voice lowering.

The Ryles are not joyless. Far from it. They have reacquainted themselves with pleasure. They feel less guilt. But it is not an either/or proposition. The shadow of grief recedes, but is rarely vanquished. While they can experience pleasure, they are still suspicious of it. But they make and receive jokes — are fluent with wit, irony, and sarcasm. It is like dismemberment, a favoured analogy of Fran's. The absence of Rebecca and its effects can never be reversed. But with time, they have adapted. It started with acceptance.

A year-and-a-half passed before I saw the Ryles again. They were in Melbourne this time, visiting the city for the first time. We met at my favourite pub, 'my home away from home,' I told them dumbly, and where I had written a fair amount of this book. As we had in Perth, we riffed and reminisced enjoyably, oiled by pints of lager. They looked good — they're a handsome couple. Marie wore a dress, and Fran a neat sweater over a collared shirt. His grey hair was cropped short; he'd 'been to a Lebanese barber' earlier that day. Fran puffed on his cigarillos; Marie, on her tailored cigarettes. My fondness for them was immediately reinforced.

One big thing had just happened; another was just months away. 'Did you know Duggan was knocked back for parole?' Marie asked me. I didn't, and was stunned. I had assumed, in fact, that the parole hearings wouldn't be held for months. 'He'll come back up for it in three years.'

They were relieved, obviously. They had submitted statements about the effect his release would have on the family, and resubmitted their victim impact statements that were ignored at the original trial. 'It was exhausting,' Marie said, 'but it's got to be done, right? We don't know why he got blocked, do we?' She turned to Fran.

Families aren't notified of the reasons for parole decisions, merely the outcome. But they had their suspicions. 'We were in the taxi to the airport to come here,' Marie said, 'and we heard that there'd been a riot at Albany prison,' where Duggan is kept.

'I did sort of think, *Oh, I wonder if he's been bludgeoned to death,*' Fran said in his gently guilty way.

The WA Department of Corrective Services confirmed that 20 prisoners had trashed parts of the prison and then barricaded themselves in a room for hours. After their surrender, 15 prisoners were transferred. The Ryles wondered if Duggan had been one of the riotous inmates, and firmly suspected as much when the department notified them that Duggan had been transferred back to the higher-security Casuarina Prison in Perth.

It startled me, and reminded me of what Luke Richards, the petrol-station attendant, had told me when we met. Richards had described Duggan the night of the murder as scrawny, but was shocked to see him when he testified nearly two years later in court. Duggan was much bigger; he'd been working out. That was in 2006, so what had these additional eight years of prison done to him? He had routinely ignored my letters. I only knew the stories of him from before he went to jail. How big was he now? And how large was his understanding of what he had done?

The other big thing that Fran and Marie told me was that they would soon be marking their 30th wedding anniversary. I was impressed. I had seen married couples lose a child, and then divorce. It was a compounding misery, as each became an awful mirror of the other's suffering. Or sometimes the demons that the death bore were too much for the other. But here were the Ryles, wandering around Melbourne, 30 years married, and Fran cajoling Marie to take a two-hour coach to Bendigo to see paintings by Turner and Constable. Fran had started a fine-arts and history degree since we'd last seen each other — the same one as his son, Chris. 'He's not bad at the art, you know,' Marie said. 'Not my cup of tea, but he's not bad.' This was in addition to his politics degree.

Fran modestly extolled the things he'd learnt in the course — and the importance of creative expression. Chris had moved out to a nearby share house, but would come back home for proper meals. Andy was still living with them. Fran and Marie were still in the same jobs — Fran as a carer, Marie as a receptionist at the local medical clinic. Fran was frustrated by the administrative load — 'the hoops the government demand you jump through' — and the fact that he spent less time than he'd like with the people who needed his help. Marie felt that he'd be better suited to social work proper. At this suggestion, Fran bowed his head. It was both a modest acknowledgment of the wisdom of Marie's suggestion, and a resignation to the fact that he had until now done little to realise it.

All of us make meaning, but we don't work as hard at it as the Ryles do. Every day, they make decisions to keep from going under. It gets easier over time, but there are pitfalls. A part of this is symbolism — they understand its power, and just as easily know its inadequacy. Each year since Rebecca's death, they have planted a memorial tree at the site of her death. And each year it has failed to prosper. Mostly the trees have died; one year they unknowingly planted a tree with poisonous leaves, and the school asked that it be replaced. But the most recent tree was deliberately snapped in half. When that happened, Fran felt the old anger surge.

For a history unit he was studying at university, Fran was asked to write about the act of commemoration. He wrote about planting a tree each year at the sacred site. He quickly saw the analogy: the young, hopeful things they planted were dying prematurely, just like their young, hopeful daughter they symbolised. But they persevere. 'It's silly, in a way, to try and replace a human being with a tree,' Fran said. 'But it's important to us.'

Fran and Marie have had their love for their sons dramatically reaffirmed, and they think hard about what that love means and how it can be best expressed. They know the importance of allowing them to grow through adventure, but are also exquisitely aware of their children's vulnerability. Regardless, they know the awesome centrality of that love in their lives.

'The world breaks everyone,' Hemingway wrote, 'and afterward many are strong at the broken places.' It's classic Hemingway — neat and resonant — but we can't take someone's strength for granted. The possibility of relapse doesn't tire. Every day there are decisions to *be* strong. It's not as simple as enjoying a mysterious, subconscious reservoir of fortitude. We are too glib in designating somebody as 'strong', as if there are only the weak and the durable fixed in distinct and permanent positions. In this case, the 'strong' will never collapse and we can relax, admiring them from afar. We fetishise endurance, and for good reason, but the reality's more complex, and impressive, than simply *existing*. For the Ryles, there's a vigilant *maintenance* of strength, a constant process. And while some are stronger than others, it is also true that we can all be both.

Fran once told me that he'd been impressed by Robert Hughes's Australian history *The Fatal Shore*. He remembers the Pebble Men. 'Hughes is talking about these guys that were on one of the hardest penal colonies,' Fran said. 'Not sure if it was Norfolk Island or not — but they were called Pebble Men. You couldn't break them. They were so abused from poverty-stricken childhoods in England. They'd been flogged, beaten, eventually sent to Australia for whatever crime. Flogged again, brutalised, starved. They got to such a state that you could just flog these guys to death. They could bleed to death, but they wouldn't crack. Wouldn't cry. One hundred lashes? So what. Pebble Men. You feel like there's not many people who can hurt you now, you've done all you can. Without being stonehearted or bitter, nothing could break me like that has done. I'm not going to be that flinty-hearted myself, but dig deep. I don't know if that makes sense to anyone.'

The simplistic interpretation here would be that

Fran is a Pebble Man. But he isn't. He hasn't traded his tenderness, curiosity, or willingness to be vulnerable. He's tough, but it's not the bleak, stony toughness of someone who has abandoned the risks and pleasures of love. Fran can take inspiration from the Pebble Men — he can be semi-confident in his capacity for suffering — but his great strength is found in his refusal to close off his heart from others, or new experiences.

Fran and Marie are both strong enough to know, simultaneously, that life is both brutal *and* warm, filled with suffering *and* pleasure, and that the open secret is to pursue more life, not less, even when you're scarred. Theirs isn't a *carpe diem* exuberance. They aren't sprinting into the fray. They're working-class English, modest and self-deprecating, and their approach is still marked by sensitivity, fear, and cynicism. They still scream and cry. But they haven't given up — and they haven't changed dramatically. They're still open; they haven't succumbed to bitter nihilism. They know the worst, but still accept that life can be good — a different kind of good, dimmed by what happened, but good nonetheless.

As I write, the tenth anniversary of Rebecca's death is two days away. The family are sick with anticipation. Anniversaries are excruciating, and the fact of it being a decade will not seem arbitrary to them. They will think of the passing of time, the changes since Rebecca's death, and how she is frozen in their minds as the vivacious teenager who left the house to meet friends that night. 'I think she would've been a nurse, if she were still alive,' Marie told me. 'Probably with children. She loved kids.'

Many of the students enrolled at Mindarie Primary School when Rebecca was killed will now have graduated from high school. Some would have graduated from university, or started families of their own. And in their place, running around the murder site on the anniversary, will be new kids — some of them not yet alive when James walked Rebecca to the park.

AFTERWORD

Why did I write this book? You might suppose by its
title that I hoped to triumphantly improve upon the
experts' failure to find a motive. But I didn't, and I never
could have. That would have required an insight and
access that I never acquired. What initially resonated
was my brother's proximity to Duggan and, by
extension, my own. Our suburban adolescence shared
much. But then I met the Ryles, and found brave and
lucid narrators of a suffering we rarely observe with
care. With this in mind, I had grown contemptuous of
popular treatments of criminality. My publisher felt the
same, and was at first reluctant about my proposal. His
thinking was simple: much crime writing is salacious
and vampiric, and elides the fact that there is often very
little interesting about the people who attract infamy.
We passionately absorb the graphic particulars and
ignore the rest. It is an old concern.

—

In 2013, I went to work for the chief commissioner of Victoria Police as a senior advisor and speechwriter, and I made my first mistake before I'd even begun. Following a long discussion with the chief before I'd signed my contract, I knew my first task would be a graduation speech to the force's newest members. I asked him for previous examples, and if he could recommend any histories of Victoria Police. As it was, he gave me one: Bob Haldane's scholarly *The People's Force*.

Haldane was a former Victorian detective, and a graduate of the FBI academy. He was also the first Victorian police officer to receive a PhD — the book I was now reading on the tram home from Police Headquarters was his doctoral work. With the help of Haldane I could begin historicising these fresh constables — placing them within 160 years of institutional existence. I underlined passages about the messy conception of Victoria Police, the troubled reliance on convicts to enforce nascent laws. The formation of civic society is slow and impure, and for a long while the force was a nest of illiterate drunks. Haldane was uninterested in forging grand origin myths for Victoria Police. Here it was in its long and difficult birth. *This I can work with*, I thought.

Enter Ned Kelly. Police corruption and militancy played out among frontiersmen and criminals, and a national myth emerged. In Haldane's descriptions of the outlaw era, he quotes Kelly from his famous Jerilderie letter of 1879. Of Victorian police, Kelly wrote ungrammatically, '... big ugly fat-necked wombat headed big bellied magpie legged narrow hipped splay-footed sons of Irish bailiffs or english landlords which is better known as Officers of Justice or Victorian Police who some call honest gentlemen'.

No doubt these words were hot and vulgar when written, but time had worn away their edges. We were left with the daintiness of aged profanity. I scribbled down Kelly's lines in my draft speech, allowing for the chief to mock-warn the graduates that in 2013 they would be called much worse in the streets. As humour it was lame, and I marked the lines for possible removal, but conversely I thought the remark went some way in replacing the mechanical platitudes of previous speeches. Perhaps it was a small step in restoring some warmth to these commencement addresses. I left them in.

I shouldn't have. Once I'd officially started work, the chief called me into his office. He was gentle, but firm. 'Never,' he said, 'mention Kelly in a speech again.'

I was chastened. I knew that Kelly had murdered police. I knew that right up until the end, right before he swung by his neck, Kelly cursed cops. But nor did I think that my borrowing Kelly's words valorised him, that I was attempting some subversive invocation of the man.

I was naive. I had read Kelly's words and been struck by them aesthetically — how colourful they were, how time had drained their danger. I had made a stylistic choice at odds with the long and galvanising memory of Victoria

Police members, and in doing so I had committed a cardinal sin of speechwriting: I had misjudged the audience.

As much as I believed that quoting Kelly's diatribe didn't constitute an endorsement of the man, one fact remained: Kelly had been a cop-killer. Sergeant Kennedy and Constables Lonigan and Scanlon were still dead. To mention Kelly at the 'heart' of Victoria Police — the Glen Waverley academy — was profane. I had learnt my lesson.

This institutional hatred is not only of Kelly, but our contemporary celebration of him. The collective feeling of Victoria Police is set not only upon elevating the dignity of the slain officers, but on questioning our iconic regard for a killer. The average Victoria Police member argues that in the wider culture's embrace of a martyr, we're blithely forgiving the unforgivable. Is our celebration of Kelly our id's way of rebelling against our dull lawfulness? When former footballer Ben Cousins had Kelly's final words, 'Such is life', tattooed on his chiselled abdomen, was he claiming for himself some of the fetishised iconoclasm of the outlaw?

I am sympathetic to the police attitude towards Kelly, and my sympathy extends to their repulsion of modern thugs being transformed into celebrities. A police officer I worked with once told me a story about the ex-wife of a gangland assassin. While this officer was in the company of the woman, she complained about being constantly stopped in shopping malls by strangers wanting photos and autographs. The officer suspected that her ostensible lament was really boastfulness. It happens all the time in Melbourne — figures of the underworld being fêted by strangers on sidewalks. One sees Mick Gatto comfortably reclined at a city café, smug in his aura of crookedness, and one sees punters clamouring to shake his hand. It is a repugnant spectacle.

The TV series *Underbelly* testifies powerfully to our glib attraction to criminality. Each new series of the show is stunningly cleansed of shade and consequence, determinedly emptied of the banality that characterises most thugs. *Underbelly* lacquers bastards with mystique, and covers the stench of nihilism with toilet freshener. Cops rightly despise it. We all should.

I've interviewed a few violent criminals, and in my experience neither their stark inner lives nor their crimes are terribly interesting in themselves. But if the success of *Underbelly* tells us anything, it's that we'll almost always choose entertainment over instruction. We might not know it, but we're debasing the victims and ourselves in the process. We're privileging the crime over its consequences, and almost committing a posthumous trespass upon the dead by finding them interesting only because of what happened to them. Only in death have they become alive to us.

To watch *Underbelly*'s saturated colour schemes, slick cuts, supple flesh, and bold graphics is to see ancient questions of evil, sin, redemption, and justice turned into music videos. We are treating our souls like chewing gum. This witless enthusiasm for thugs is a triumph of the hyper-real, the way pop culture smears Vaseline on the borders of the real and our representations of the real. We permit pop culture to elevate the subjects of TV drama into soap stars themselves. We are cannibalising our culture and our own judgement if our adoration of entertainment replaces moral evaluation. If we can no longer distinguish between false, artful treatments of murder and the putrid reality — we're stuffed.

This is something that David Chase, the melancholy creator of the hit TV series *The Sopranos*, understands. In mob boss Tony Soprano, Chase created a murderous villain whose inner life *was* interesting, but principally because Chase was determined to map the moral and emotional corollaries of Tony's violence and treachery.

Tony Soprano sits uneasily atop a bloody mountain, and when he sleeps, his subconscious surveys the land below — the ghosts of friends he's murdered, and the promise of more. During the day he seeks therapy, and medicates himself with booze and nostalgia, TV and anti-depressants. It's far from glamorous. In fact, it's perfectly wretched.

Regardless, fans of the show began valorising this beast. Chase was perplexed by them, and then disgusted. By cheering Tony on, were we vicariously cheering a man bravely shredding the social contract? Chase wondered. As Tony became increasingly blood-crazed — as his trespasses became more sickening — Chase seemed to be trying to slap our fondness for him from our hands. When Tony murdered his nephew, you could hear Chase admonishing us as clearly as you could hear Christopher Moltisanti gurgle in his death throes. 'He's evil, remember? Give up your love for him.'

Among fans of *The Sopranos*, a sickly conflation was struck between *interesting* and *likeable*, a baffling arrangement given that Tony and his crew were deathly and piggish. They were destroyers, not creators, and their celebration of America's Italian immigration became a sort of sick joke — theirs was a nightmare version of the American Dream, using intimidation to parasitically extract from the real work of others.

Our interest in crime — and the stories we tell about it — are often puerile quests for vicarious thrill-seeking, but there's another force that shapes it: denial. We are so deeply invested in believing it will never happen to us that we are constantly imagining the complicity of the victims of violent crime. Murdered sex worker? Comes with the job. Bludgeoned wife? White trash. Young rape victim? Slutty booze-hound. In our minds, we effortlessly solve open murders by apportioning blame to the victim, and we do this because we cannot stomach the thought that it might happen to us. In conferring blame, we subtly congratulate ourselves for our superior judgement, a judgement that ensures that we will avoid the worst. But in doing this we are injuring our imaginations — the lifeblood of sympathy — and misapprehending the nature of violence.

—

Why did James Duggan murder Rebecca Ryle? I have been unable to dismiss my brother's judgement. 'He definitely had problems,' Cameron said. 'He was very angry. You could see that his upbringing and everything that had happened had built on and on. You could see it getting worse in him. Probably one of the angriest people I've ever known. And for that reason I can see him snapping and doing it. Maybe Rebecca rejected him, and that was the final rejection, after being rejected by friends. I remember being really young, and him sort of having crushes on girls and them not liking him. I think he was constantly faced with rejection. I would say that was the main issue.'

There were rumours that Duggan had been mocked at The Boat that night for his presumed virginity. Perhaps he was sexually rebuffed by Rebecca, and her reaction to his advances therefore became doubly intolerable to him. But see how bloated with qualifiers these sentences are? The whole story is.

In contemplating my adolescence — and my brother's — I returned to the crippling ironies of Duggan's scene. To be strong, you had to meekly follow. To be distinguished was to show fealty to a system of violence. To demonstrate physical bravery was to forfeit moral courage. The psychological comforts of gang membership were perilous in their contradictions. The organising principles were seductive, but ruinous to individual growth and self-reckoning. The collective desire to be *seen* to be tough belittled genuine fortitude.

'James was always weird around girls.' I heard variations of this line throughout my research. I never knew what to do with it, other than to treat it as a small fire, the smoke from which infiltrated my appraisal of his crime.

My appraisal is this: Duggan was serially frustrated by his inability to impose his will on the world. The few times he could — via vandalism and petty theft — were cheap and petulant demonstrations of power, ones which often diminished his social standing when practised against friends. An emotionally confused young man, the frustration ossified and became to him evidence, not of his flaws, but of the essential meanness of the world. Duggan looked sourly outwards, not bravely inwards, and there was a muddling of cause and effect encouraged by the idiocies of his gang conscription.

It was the same with women. Their indifference became proof of this universal injustice. Duggan's supposed virginity cruelled his social status in a culture of sexual obsession and entitlement. That Duggan was bitter, charmless, and drifting would have affected his relations with young women, but I suspect he viewed their rejections — subtle or otherwise — as the work of a feminine conspiracy, rather than of his own inadequacies. Not gifted with self-awareness or supportive friends, Duggan might have brooded upon the prison that 'the world' — that vague but endlessly reinforcing construction — had consigned him to. Rather than study the actual design and dimensions of his cell, Duggan sought to make his captivity more comfortable with booze and dope. Soon the metaphorical prison would be conjoined with an actual one. If I am right about this, it was yet another irony that eluded him. I am convinced that the imperilled status of male expression in this environment contributed to his criminality.

Over the past two years, I have thought often of the Australian film *Somersault*. Set in Jindabyne, in NSW's ski fields, it's a meditatively slow drama about — in part — the ruinous consequences of male anxiety and inarticulateness. Modest lives are played out in the snowfields, where the grey sky and snowfall is the perfect backdrop for its characters' melancholic drift. It also serves as an appropriate analogue for their frozen interior lives. At the local pub, lust, loyalty, and disappointment are expressed in grunts and shrugs. There's a depth of feeling, but everyone is caged by a profound inability — or unwillingness — to voice it.

We don't lament the characters' inarticulacy because it's an assault on the pleasures of eloquence. We lament it because it's dangerous. Each grunt is a self-laceration, a deferred revelation, another step towards isolation. Tempests of regret and confusion go unrelieved. I'm not talking about vocabulary here, though that helps. It's more the cultural failure to develop a habit of expression, however laconic. This is less about education and the quality of speech than it is about a particular masculine self-consciousness about developing, and articulating, self-awareness. In *Somersault*'s world, longing and loathing are to be disastrously quelled or physically transposed. It seems that in this small town everyone knows everyone, but everyone's alone.

Like most things, we tend towards an unhelpful either/or duality on this, irritably defending one of the following two propositions: that male reticence is boorish and harmful, or that the new emphasis on expression is narcissistic — a preference for self-absorption over strength.

The problem with both propositions is that they're stubbornly absolute. They're examples of faith, not analysis. Behind each is a dogma: that enlightenment may follow expression, or that grace is found in silence. The reality is that both can be true simultaneously.

The unworkable idea of the British stiff upper lip kept coming up in most conversations I had with Fran and Marie. In my life and theirs, it was an abiding theme, something that blighted our respective family trees. Marie once again raised the brutality of Fran's father's emotional distance, which Fran politely accepted. 'We keep talking about this, don't we?' he asked rhetorically, sipping his ale.

'It's a feature in your family stories, and mine,' I said. 'These sorts of perversions which come from a refusal to talk about stuff. I'm sure the Brits don't have a monopoly on this, but our worship of the Greatest Generation's stoicism keeps being dirtied by our own stories.'

'It's true, innit?' Fran said. 'If you read histories of

England during the Blitz, there's this great Spirit of Britain. And there was. But history is written by the victors, isn't it, and there was also petty crime, looting, and the exploitation of kids in homes. It's not black and white. Like my father's life. I was in Antarctica when I heard he'd died. I got a message to call home, and somehow I just knew. The last ten years were not good with him, I think he went down the wrong road. But he could be creative and thoughtful. And you know, I miss him.'

In many conversations over many months, each one charmingly candid, we returned to the damage wrought by the emotional obstinacy of family elders. We unfurled our separate histories, and the pains of British inarticulacy became clear. Fran's father's silence wasn't strength — it was a punishing weakness masquerading as discipline. And it burnt his children. Marie could also cite examples of damaging silences and secret-keeping, things which maintained echoes throughout the lineage.

Like Fran's dad, my grandfather was brutalised in the Second World War, albeit far more directly as a prisoner of the Japanese. It was a bitter fact for my grandfather that the ship's voyage — the one freighting him to war, departing from Albany and winding its way east along the Bight and then upwards to the South-East Asian theatre — eclipsed the time spent fighting. Within weeks he was captured.

In fairness to my grandfather, it's right that I precede a description of his behaviour post-war with an outline of what happened when he was captive in it. While patrolling a jungle, Robert's unit was overwhelmed by Japanese troops and condemned to squalid prisoner camps. He was starved and beaten in Changi, and deployed later to hammer sleepers on the Thai–Burma railway. He and his mates became ghouls, malnourished and stained with jungle sores. They subsisted on filthy rice, and filled troughs with diarrhoea. Attrition was high. If the malnutrition, dysentery, or septicaemia didn't get them, there were always the summary executions.

A precious object in my family is the notebook my grandfather secretly maintained in the camp. Its contents are extraordinary. In spidery script, he pencilled details of atrocities — one page includes a description of the heads of executed prisoners impaled on spikes — alongside the lyrics and chords of love songs. On one page, my grandfather has painstakingly written the words and guitar positions for a Bing Crosby song. 'Where the blue of the night meets the gold of the day, someone waits for me/and the gold of her hair crowns the blue of her eyes like a halo, tenderly.' There are many similar treatments of other pop songs in the notebook.

The script had to be tiny to conserve the sheets. On a few pages, you can see him practising musical notation; on others, he's learning shorthand — 'the vowel is written on the inside of a curve.' On one page, he has written Berile's 'Five Basic Principles of Gag Formula':

1. Comedian is butt of joke
2. Audience are let into joke before actors

3. Comedy is derived from misery or frustration
4. Comedy is based on malapropisms —
   mispronounced words, etc.
5. Comedian is 'smart Alec' — as if he is above audience.

It was to stave off boredom, we assume, which must have been extreme because the discovery of the diary would have resulted in a severe beating. At the very least.

He returned psychically bent. My grandfather was violent, selfish, and furiously insolent, and he remained that way until he died half a century later.

Not even my father, who had adopted his own traits of parental authoritarianism for a while, would accept as healthy or useful the earlier behaviour of my grandfather. My uncle Greg had developed an early passion for music, which manifested itself in some surprising adventures. Well before celebrities attracted shells of bodyguards, my uncle insinuated himself into the lives of numerous rock stars. Staking out Perth Airport when the Rolling Stones made their first Australian visit in 1965, Greg secreted himself in the luggage hold of the band's coach. He listened as people boarded, and then as the engine rumbled to life. Then he waited. After a while, he pushed open the hatch and emerged into the aisle of the bus to greet Jagger, Richards, and company. Maybe it's an indication of the times, or the druggy generosity of the Stones, that my uncle wasn't beaten and dumped by the road. Instead, he was welcomed to a seat, and received an impromptu harmonica lesson from Mick Jagger. The next day, my uncle drove Keith Richards down to

Mandurah in his Beetle. He left with some great stories, as well as a signed sleeve of the Stones' first LP and Jagger's harmonica.

It didn't end there. Greg scaled the drainpipe at Roy Orbison's hotel, and was rewarded with an amiable chat with the singer. He left with Orbison's belt. Sneaking backstage at a Kinks concert, Greg was employed as the lighting director for the remainder of the band's tour. He collected guitar picks and set-lists.

Whether it was due to ingenuity or obsession, Greg compiled an impressive collection of memorabilia, much of it very valuable. But his father didn't see it that way. Greg's passion, and its affectations — long hair and boots — were a vulgar affront to my grandfather. Greg was ordered to cut his hair into a military-style crew-cut, and one night, while Greg was out, his father lit a bonfire in the backyard. Jagger's harmonica, Orbison's belt, the Kinks set-list, and most of his records were cremated.

My only memory of my grandfather is a brutal row he had with my father, punctuated by a slammed door. My father had confronted him about his indifference to us, his family. 'I don't give a stuff about your kids,' he yelled. And that was that — I never saw him again.

It is tempting to view all this as a terrible clash of generations — of hopelessly scarred elders and their spoilt children, ungratefully enjoying the tranquillity their fathers bequeathed them. But the story's more complicated. My grandfather was involved in a fight in a car park not long after the war. It resulted in him falling and cracking his head. It is said that he changed afterwards, that it worsened his aggression. Couple that with a near-absence of psychological help for our veterans — the near-absence of an understanding of trauma — and you have something more than an avatar of generational suffering.

But linked to all of this are expectations of masculinity, ones that were sternly championed by my grandfather, passionately rejected by my uncle, and aggressively reinforced in turn. They were lessons more deeply absorbed by my father, I think, than by his younger brother.

The causes of this inarticulacy are myriad, but it's the consequences that are important here. Damaged inner lives were worsened by silence, expressed obliquely in acts of savagery, internalised by children, and unwittingly shared with their own. My father, to his great credit, is unlearning many of those lessons.

The Ryles considered themselves generational circuit-breakers. Or, to conscript a different metaphor, they had turned themselves into a dam wall, separating their boys from the rough waters of family history. From here, things will be different.

For all the detectives, and lawyers, and the battery of psychological examination, I have only a communion with my own past to attempt to explain what was in Duggan's head when he left The Boat with Rebecca. What follows is speculative.

James went to The Boat that night, and spent his dole money on beer. He bought jugs, and emptied them heroically. The sad idleness of the day was replaced with gusto. He mocked strangers, and exalted in Gareth's stupidity. The beer and melee relieved the boredom. But he listened terribly. Others discussed work, but, lacking ambition and prospects, he was listless and intimidated. It would not be the night to be reminded of such things.

There was word of a car trip up the coast to a club, and he glimpsed himself as socially mobile, alluringly dashing from one party to the next. Plus, he needed to get laid. It was barren here. That's what he told himself, anyway. Sexual prospects were always over the horizon, always at the next place. It was the optimism of delusion, an extension of the logic that there was something cruel and obstinate about 'the world'; but if he was persistent enough, he'd crack through. His luck would come — maybe at this club, or the one after. Anyway, if he was in perpetual pursuit, he'd never have to stop and consider himself.

But they weren't taking him. He wasn't catching that lift. Story of his life. And yet, here was this chick. Smiling, trustful, attentive. Attractive, too. She smoked, seemed cool. Fuck, she was talking to him. He was in. There weren't many friends left to boast to these days, but he could picture telling Gareth. *What a night, man. You got in a fucking fight — and I got some.* Duggan's brain was lit with libidinous anticipation, but perhaps a distant, pre-verbal recognition was humming in his frontal lobe:

sex might serve as a ceasefire in his spiteful relations with 'the world'. Might dilute a pattern of poisonous self-recrimination. Do thoughts exist without vocabulary? Did Duggan dimly intuit this significance?

Whatever. Here she was. Rebecca. No doubt she had been impressed with his swagger. He didn't give a fuck. He was fun. Courageous. Cool. But, fuck, he was drunk. Maybe he was misinterpreting her attention. Duggan wasn't used to accepting female geniality as just that. It was a sign of desire, right? That's how the boys up this way saw it. As prelude.

She was still here. He'd walk her home. That was another good sign. Gareth had bailed, hilariously. What a fucking guy. And now Rebecca needed to go to the bathroom, and he was waiting expectantly on the boardwalk. What was that? Some geek cunt was saying something to him. Fuck does he think he is? 'Fuck you say?'

Then the police arrived, and Duggan watched the pigs enter the pub. He had a vivid hatred of them. Fuckers were too late, though. Gareth was long gone, plus they were looking for Liam now. Duggan smiled at his ingenuity. Liam was a fake pussy. Fuck him. But maybe somewhere in his brain another recognition was slowly forming: that he was still trying to distinguish himself by fighting everything.

So the two were crossing the car park, and Duggan saw his mate's shoe. He didn't have many mates, so he grabbed it, grateful for this sign of blokey fraternity in front of Rebecca. It suggested other larrikin adventures, other friends, a long line forward and back of warm and collegial conspiracies. She couldn't know that that line didn't exist, knew him only as he was now, full of piss and vigour. But, fuck, he was doubtful. And the resentment was always close. The defensive hostility. The dull headache that settles when you're always blaming someone or something. Fuck it. He was getting laid.

And here was Gareth's second shoe, and they were having fun now. It was Hansel and Gretel. The night was cool, but not cold. The streets were quiet. Rebecca was almost home. She had school tomorrow.

And then they were in the park. It was dark, but the encircling streetlights shared a little illumination. Rebecca could just make out her house. Had she checked her phone? There were messages there, but they'd all be asleep. Rebecca's parents had worked so hard to bring them here. And there was wisdom to it. Aspiration.

It was more an oval than a park, ringed shallowly with young trees. Quiet now, but on school days filled with thin limbs chasing things. You could see the sand among the turf. It was all built on sand. But you couldn't see that now. Not at night.

So what does James do now but make his move? He didn't get that lift to the club, but it hasn't been a bad night. He's stared that dude down, given the cops a bum steer to help Gareth. And now here he is with a girl. It *is* his night. Adventures. Just like Jay and Silent Bob. So he tries to kiss her, stumbling, inelegant, stinking, but fuck it … And — Rebecca pulls back. She's shaking her head.

Embarrassed. Apologetic. She makes an immediate audit, almost as swift as light, of whatever there could be in her behaviour to attract such attention. But just as swiftly, Duggan's mind compiles a dismal collage of past rejections, and suddenly Rebecca's friendliness looks like a trap. Just another agent sent for his humiliation. 'She was too trusting,' her parents will say, but she has simply trusted that openness won't be confused for betrayal. Trusted that sharing a cigarette and a walk home won't ensnare her in a stranger's pathology.

Duggan's head is a steam engine. Every input confirms its bias: that 'the world' is calculating against him. Especially women. Fuck them. And the engine is hissing now, unrelieved by imagination, reflection, or expression. The pressure has been building for ages. Years. Now it's falling apart. He grabs her, places her in a chokehold. And everything is just spinning around and around and around and around.

We know these 'things' are spinning for a very long time — at least three minutes. These 'things' are as large as they are apparently undiscoverable to him. In murder, James has finally communed with the depths of his rage.

James loosens his grip, and Rebecca falls to the ground, unconscious. She's not dead, but dying. No one knows when she died. Not precisely. Not even James. Is she still breathing? Probably. Shallowly. Imperceptibly. But breathing. And James is still spinning in the sand and shadows. The reckoning hasn't come yet. The anger is undiminished. Violence has given him control. But these aren't larrikin adventures anymore. Even he knows that. This is something else.

And Rebecca lies still, and James's heart is spastic, and he looks at her, and there it is again: that once elusive thing, control. Why did she lead him on? Why did she do that? He didn't have to do this. It could have gone another way. Is she dead? He's not sure. But he's never seen a naked woman before. Not in the flesh. This is his chance, isn't it? She won't remember it.

And she'll wake up, right? Later. But now he has her. Captive. She shouldn't have done that. And he crouches and pulls her pants off. No resistance. Pink underwear. James stares. His excitement increases. Did he *ever* know he was capable of this? Were there faint signals of distress he'd previously ignored, crushed? But he doesn't think about that now. It will come later. Maybe. Now he's thinking about what lies beneath the knickers. He struggles with her dead weight, pulling hard. Done. He flings them aside. Stares. Now he lifts the bra. It's troublesome. He should probably leave. He's ringed by small roads. Empty roads, but still. He's nervous. He takes a fifty-dollar note from her purse, and some earrings. It's instinctual. Atavistic. He takes her phone, too. That might be evidence. He's panicking. How to clear up the site? How to give the cops another bum steer? He's forgotten about Liam now. He's forgotten about a lot. This selective theft strikes him as vaguely clever, a disruption of a crime scene that will confuse police. Right now, he's an über-crook. Exercising control.

Expertly manipulative. Fuck the pigs.

He jogs. Past Rebecca's house, then right onto his stepfather's street. He drops her phone down the drain. It seems smart. They won't find that. He's fucking with them. He's in control.

But none of it is clever. He's leaving a trail of evidence. He's taking the crime scene with him. And he's going to the petrol station. A place where he'll spend her money, discard her earrings, dump her DNA, and give his real name. His fingerprints are everywhere. He's attracting witnesses. But, no. He's clever. And his brain now contains awesome contradictions, a blaze of power and shame: adrenaline, and stupidity, and a seductive sense of his own invulnerability and deftness. It's a hot mess, but when he gets to the servo he's blokey and inquisitive. His powers of manipulation are grossly exaggerated — but they exist. 'Mate, I need a taxi,' he tells Luke Richards.

For 45 minutes, Richards indulges a bore, not a monster. Then the taxi arrives and takes James to his bed for the final time. The Ryles are all asleep.

Even after assuming a novelist's licence, after unshackling myself from the established record, I cannot render the unclothing of Rebecca with any confidence. My imagination doesn't stir. It shrinks. Perhaps it's emaciated. Untrained and slovenly. But it's also intimidated before something so alien, so darkly inscrutable. The justice system couldn't divine an explanation. Nor would Duggan provide one. And nor will my imagination.

And I suspect it's because James Duggan made little sense to himself.

Did the law of averages simply offer up Duggan as the vilest product of suburban banality? Or was he always secretly aberrant within it — chance rather than fate being the chief influence? I suspect the former. As I had when I was 23. But I don't know.

More importantly, the Ryles don't know. Not entirely. They formed explanations — whittled them from hate, facts, desperation, and need. But they were never satisfactory. They had to creep, bleeding, towards comprehension. And then they crept towards something else — a rejection of 'irritable certainty' as well as a commitment to restoring sense and stability to their lives. The reader might demand the pleasures of resolution. But the Ryles work with accepting its opposite.

ACKNOWLEDGEMENTS

I am indebted to the Ryle family for their trust, candour, and hospitality. You generously gave a part of your nervous systems, and this book would not exist without it. You will not be forgotten.

The fact of this book is also attributable to my beautiful partner, Stel — thank you for years of patient support, proofreading, and thoughtful suggestions — as it is to my publishers, Scribe, who plucked me from obscurity and took a punt. Thanks to Henry, Marika, and Julia.

I am also grateful to my parents, who loaned me the money for a very expensive court transcript, and never erred in their interest in my project; and my brothers Cameron and Howard, who gave me a lot of their time to explore our pasts. And to my late uncle Greg, a man possessed of stories that spellbound my friends and me.

I'm also indebted to talented friends, who read and adroitly edited this work. Nick Tapper, you are a wizard. Thanks also to Erik Jensen and Dave Landauer.

Thanks to the police officers I met in the office of the chief commissioner — I learnt a lot.

Thanks also to the large number of people I spoke to for this book. Not all of you feature in it, but I'm appreciative of the time you gave me. You shared your history, intelligence, expertise, and time. Without that, there would have been no book.

Finally, cheers to the Standard Hotel for the agreeable office.

Fran and Marie Ryle would like to thank the countless people — friends and strangers alike — who offered them their hearts and minds in their time of anguish. The Ryles remain touched by the past counsel of loved ones, police, and the wider community. Their gratitude endures.